Nicaraguan Peasant Poetry from Solentiname

Nicaraguan Peasant Poetry from Solentiname

Translated with an Introduction by David Gullette

West End Press
1988

Thanks are due to a number of people who helped me refine and improve this book: Carlo Baldi, Yolanda Blanco, Carol Sanchez Costello, Mariita Guevara, Sean Gullette, George Moore, doña Lolita Ramírez, Alejandro Ramírez, doña Natalia Sequeira, doña Olivia Silva, and the people of Isla Felipe Peña.

Special gratitude to Ernesto Cardenal, who encouraged this project from its inception; Mary Jane Treacy, who checked the translation for correctness; and the Simmons College Fund for Research, whose grant allowed me to travel to Solentiname.

Our thanks to Paul Lauter for donating the photograph of his painting from Solentiname for our cover illustration.

ISBN 0-931122-48-1

West End Press, Box 27334, Albuquerque, NM 87125

Table of Contents

Consciousness, Poetry and Rebellion:
The Peasant Poets of Solentiname,
by David Gullette 1

Nicaraguan Peasant Poetry
from Solentiname (Texts) 23

Felipe Peña 24
Elvis Chavarría 48
Dónald Guevara 60
Bosco Centeno 66
Gloria Guevara 90
Iván Guevara 100
Pedro Pablo Meneses 124
Alejandro Guevara 136
Nubia Arcia 138
William Guevara 144
Esperanza Guevara 146
Myriam Guevara 148
Natalia Sequeira 154
Elena Pineda 160
Olivia Silva 162
Eddy Chavarría 172
Julia Chavarría 180
Irene Agudelo 182
José Ramón Meneses 184
Mauricio Chavarría 186
Jonny Chavarría 188
Juan Agudelo 190

Appendix 195

Glossary 203

Short Bibliography 209

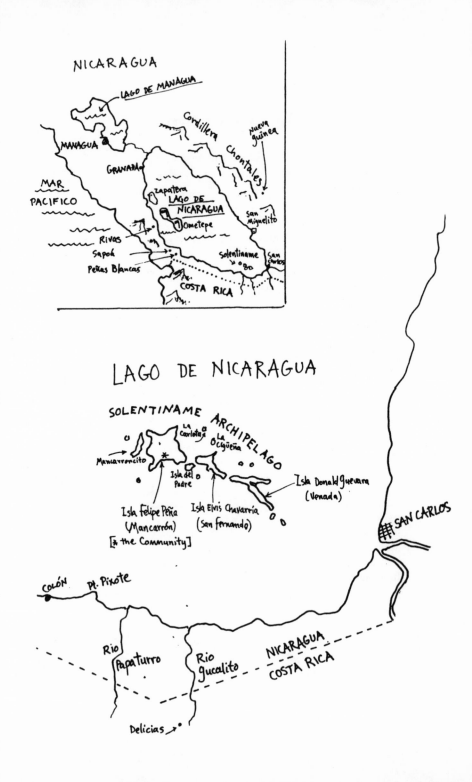

Consciousness, Poetry and Rebellion:
The Peasant Poets of Solentiname

CONSCIOUSNESS, POETRY, AND REBELLION: THE PEASANT POETS OF SOLENTINAME

> Learning to read and write ought to be an opportunity for men to know what *speaking the word* really means: a human act implying reflection and action. As such it is a primordial human right and not the privilege of a few. Speaking the word is not a true act if it is not at the same time associated with the right of self-expression and world-expression, of creating and re-creating, of deciding and choosing and ultimately participating in society's historical process.
>
> —Paulo Freire, *The Politics of Education*

1.

Between Lake Michigan and Lake Titicaca there is no expanse of fresh water larger than Lake Nicaragua, 100 miles from north to south and 40 miles wide, bounded on the east by the Chontales range where Eugene Hasenfus was shot down, and on the west by a series of volcanoes, including two that rise together out of the lake itself to form the island of Ometepe. Nicaraguans call the lake "El Mar Dulce"—The Sweet Sea. There are places on the western shore that are only 10 miles from the Pacific. And yet its umbilical link to the world of salt water is the Rio San Juan, a mainly navigable river that flows from San Carlos at the southeast corner of the lake all the way to San Juan del Norte on the Caribbean. Occasionally the surface of the lake is broken by the passing of the *sábalo real* or giant tarpon (current record stands at 120 lbs.) or the bull sharks that at some point in the lake's history made their way upriver and adapted to fresh water. The visitor slowly chugging down the lake from Granada to San Carlos on the *Gustavo Orozco*—a big clean modern boat, gift to the people of Nicaragua from the people of the Netherlands—peers over the rail into dark milky-green water rich with nutrients but full of hidden dangers. The great Nicaraguan poet Pablo Antonio Cuadra, in a poem about the mythical lake-mariner Cifar, says the hero's mother gave birth to him in a boat near the island called Zapatera, and that sharks and tarpon circled the boat, "attracted by the blood."

A hundred years ago Lake Nicaragua was a hot topic in Washington and New York. Fearing European control of the newly proposed isthmian canal, in 1884 the United States government signed the Frelinghuysen-Zavala Treaty with Nicaragua whereby the U.S. would build a canal up the Rio San Juan, across the lake, and through the thin land mass separating the lake and the Pacific; Nicaragua would pay no construction costs; the canal would be jointly owned and operated. But when in January of the following year the treaty came up in the Senate for a ratification vote it failed: 32 pro vs. 23 con, about five votes short of the two-thirds needed. It would not be the last time the future of Nicaragua would be determined by a close vote in the U.S. Congress.

Despite the setback, the idea was kept alive by a group of private investors in New York who formed the Nicaragua Canal Association and in 1887 gained concessions from the Nicaraguan government to do surveys and begin laying out the route.

Congress got into the act again in 1889 by incorporating the (still private) Maritime Canal Corporation of Nicaragua, which began work in June of that year, starting at the Atlantic side, spending $4.5 million to excavate, clear land, and lay 11 miles of railroad track in the direction of the lake. The work went on until 1893 when the financial disturbances of that year sent the MCCN into bankruptcy. All work on the canal was suspended.

In the '90s the Nicaragua Canal idea surfaced a few more times in Congress, but the creation of the Isthmian Canal Commission in 1899 marked the triumph of the Panamanian alternative. Lake Nicaragua would be left to the big-finned fish and the few peasant farmers and fisherfolk who lived along its shores and on some of the islands scattered here and there.

2.

On one such group of islands, the Solentiname archipelago at the southern end of the lake, an experiment in communal self-transformation took place in the 1970s involving a remarkable fusion of poetry, painting, religion and revolution.

The seminal figure in this story is the poet Ernesto Cardenal, currently the Nicaraguan Minister of Culture, who lived in Solentiname for 12 crucial years between 1965 and 1977. Born in 1925 to a prominent family in conservative Granada, Ernesto had the usual upper-middle-class experience of education in Managua and a stint in Mexico City. At the age of 23, intrigued by the verse of Eliot, Stevens, Sandburg, Frost, H. D. and Ezra Pound in Jose Coronel Urtecho's translations, he convinced his parents to let him go to New York "to learn English." For two years in the late '40s he was at Columbia, not only learning English but reading North American poetry—adding Whitman, Marianne Moore, and William Carlos Williams to his list, but concentrating on Ezra Pound, in whose poetry he saw an interweaving of history, economics, politics, personal ideology and direct quotation from actual people. Appalled by Pound's fascism and anti-Semitism, but intrigued by his attacks on capitalism, Cardenal came to see that "you could write poetry about anything." And of course by now he was writing his own verse—nothing unusual for a gentleman from a country whose national hero, Rubén Darío, was Latin America's greatest poet, and where the young men of Ernesto's generation would recite verses in the street and greet each other with the cry, *"¡Hola, poeta!"*

Back in Nicaragua in the early '50s he fell in with a group of poets, intellectuals and army officers unhappy with the repressive rule of Anastasio Somoza, Sr. The leaders of the group were Adolfo Baez Bone and Pablo Leal, but other members included Pedro Joaquin Chamorro (whose assassination 25 years later was to galvanize middle-class support for the overthrow of Somoza's son Tacho) and Arturo Cruz, former contra leader. If it seems odd that the Sandinista Minister of Culture, Cardenal, and the contra leader Cruz should have once been comrades in arms (or at least in subversive thoughts) it serves as yet another example of the degree to which Nicaragua's conflict in the 1980s is like a squabble among old friends or even family members. All three Managua dailies, two on the left and one on the right, were edited by members of the Chamorro clan. Pablo Antonio Cuadra, literary editor of *La Prensa*, is an older cousin of Ernesto Cardenal. Edgar Chamorro worked for the contras and then turned on them, giving damaging testimony against them in Washington and The Hague.

In 1954 the Baez Bone/Leal group tried to organize an insurrection against the regime. It failed miserably. The leaders were arrested and tortured: Baez Bone was castrated; Leal's tongue was cut out; the chief torturer was young Tacho Somoza, whose clothes were said to be splattered with blood. Cardenal went into hiding.

Some time in the next year or so Cardenal underwent an intense religious upheaval that can best be described as a conversion experience. He had been brought up a nominal Catholic, but now a powerful call to some sort of meditative inner life transformed him. He severed his links with the world of direct political action and the enticements of the flesh, and in 1957 was accepted into the Trappist Monastery in Gethsemane, Kentucky, where the poet/priest Thomas Merton was in residence. The two became close friends, talking about (but because of the Trappist code, not writing) poetry, and dreaming about establishing a meditative Christian commune somewhere in the Third World, among simple people. But Cardenal grew ill, partly from the physical rigors of life at Gethsemane, and after two years headed south. 1961 found him studying theology in Colombia, where the recent example of the priest-turned-guerrilla Camilo Torres gave him food for thought: was reclusive meditation in fact the best way to accomplish the Christian mission on earth?

3.

In 1965 Ernesto Cardenal turned 40 and was ordained as a Roman Catholic priest. Earlier in that year he had arrived on Mancarrón, the largest island in the Solentiname archipelago, along with two friends, William Agudelo and Carlos Alberto, to create the sort of ideal community he and Merton had envisioned.

Only a fraction of the Solentiname *campesinos* were literate—there was a small school, but schoolteachers came and went sporadically—and contact with organized religion had usually required a trip over to San Carlos on the mainland. Cardenal began to hold Sunday services, offering a simple Mass with the Eucharist and little else. But as he came to be more accepted by the community, he began a series of discussions about the meaning of specific passages in the Gospel. These exercises in communal exegesis and commentary were held either in the church after Mass or in a little hut opposite, where the churchgoers would enjoy a regular communal Sunday lunch. "Each Sunday," writes Cardenal, "we would first distribute copies of the Gospels to those who could read. There were some who couldn't, especially among the elderly and those who lived on islands far away from the school. One of those who could read best (generally a boy or a girl) would read aloud the entire passage on which we were going to comment. Then we discussed it verse by verse." At some point Cardenal realized that these dialogues about scripture, generated by uneducated but intelligent people quick to relate the Gospel to their own spiritual, social and economic experience, were too good to lose. He began to tape them, and later to transcribe and publish them. They have since been read around the world, translated into half a dozen languages. In the U.S., the Maryknoll Press, Orbis Books, has published four volumes of these dialogues as *The Gospel in Solentiname*.

The reader of these communal exercises in interpretation soon begins to identify and distinguish between various voices and attitudes. There is doña Olivia Silva, mother of the 10 Guevara children (many of whom also take part in the discussions); her remarks show both a deep patient belief in the power of love and a shrewd sense of social reality:

> I think the word of God has been very badly preached and the Church is much to blame in this. It's because the Gospel hasn't been well preached that we have a society still divided between rich and poor. There are few places like this one where the Gospel is preached and we understand it. Also, it's us poor people who understand it. Unfortunately, the rich don't come to hear it. Where the rich are, there's no preaching like that.

Her son Alejandro likes the idea of revolution as a way of reaching Christian goals; he has a sense of history. There is old Tomás Peña, illiterate but wise, and his son Felipe who speaks freely and at length, filled with a deep anger against the rich who are "living high with banquets and parties and great feasts and sprees in their clubs, all at the people's expense, wasting and squandering among a few people what belongs to everybody."

Elvis Chavarría seems to be the most visionary of the *campesinos;* his mind works in images of light and dark, he conceives of struggles between mighty forces, and he dreams of a better world: "Humanity's starting to see that light [of Christ's love for the poor]; it's the revolution that's rising up all over the world." Other voices make themselves heard as well, including other children of doña Olivia—Iván, Myriam, Gloria, William, Mariita—and Myriam's fiancé Bosco Centeno, and Laureano Mairena. The recurrent theme of the discussions is summed up by Felipe: "Jesus was coming to divide all the wealth of the world among all the people."

Of course not everyone in the islands came to the new church—some, says Cardenal, "because they had no boat, and others because they missed the devotion to the saints, to which they were accustomed. Others stayed away through the influence of anti-Communist propaganda, and perhaps also through fear." But for those who did come, life in the Mancarrón community became part of a general enlightenment. In the mid-'70s Cardenal started a painting workshop. *Campesinos* who had always taken for granted the broad lake, the giant trees, the birds of every shape and color, the straw-thatched huts, even their neighbors, now began to see these things with new eyes as they were reconceived, reshaped, re-created under the painter's brush. As one of the painters has said, "I never really saw the world until I began to paint it."

4.

Yet another avenue to awareness was opened up in 1977 with the visit to Solentiname of Cardenal's friends, the Venezuelan Antidio Cabal and his wife Mayra Jimenez. Both were poets. Jimenez had experimented successfully with children's poetry workshops in Venezuela and Costa Rica, and decided to offer one to interested *campesinos* in Solentiname. Not surprisingly, the majority of those willing to try their hands at poetry were those who had already begun to find their voices as debaters of scripture: seven of the Guevara children and their mother doña Olivia, Elvis Chavarría, his brother Eddy, and their mother Natalia, Felipe Peña (but not old Tomás), Bosco Centeno, even the Agudelo children, Juan (seven) and Irene (five), and a few newcomers, including Pedro Pablo Meneses and Nubia Arcia.

At first Mayra and the group read and commented on already published poems—by the great modern Nicaraguan poets such as Jose Coronel Urtecho (who lived not far away on a hacienda up the Rio Frio), Pablo Antonio Cuadra, the martyred Leonel Rugama, and others, as well as poems from modern North America, ancient China and elsewhere. When it came time to read poems by Cardenal, Mayra was astonished to discover that he had never offered to show the *campesinos* his poems. "I didn't think [at that time] that peasants, with such a low cultural level, could really understand anything but the simplest verse," he later confessed. By the time Cardenal began to attend the meetings of the workshop, the participants had begun to write (and rewrite) their own poems, limited in length for the most part, and confined in subject matter to the pains and joys of love, the beauties of nature, good food, music, fishing, rum, birds, and the various moods of the lake. The style of these early exercises tends to be crisp, precise and descriptive or narrative, based on experience and the five senses, not cluttered with figurative language or conceits, and while it often focuses on strong emotion, it avoids confessional anguish. Typical of this early style is Bosco Centeno's deft sketch of the egret:

An egret goes slowly by
lazily moving her wings
seeing her image
on the calm surface of the lake.

Or Elvis Chavarría's images of lake foam:

The foam flows following
the current of the lake.
White as milk fresh in the milking pail.
It flows, piles up, it looks like heaps of snow
    along the shoreline.
As it flows to Mancarrón, so it flows
to La Cigüena, then on to La Carlota:
Like great highways across the lake.

"The first poems they wrote," says Jimenez, "were discussed between the author and myself but always in the presence of other members of the group. Before long we had begun to discuss all of them in group, which is to say, with everyone pitching in about what was good and what seemed less good. Sooner or later the author might defend his or her position, changes would be suggested, and on more than one occasion, the first draft would be entirely eliminated and replaced with a new version." Cardenal was deeply impressed by the quality of the verse being produced by these newly literate *campesinos*, many of whom had had their first experience of poetry only a few months before. It was, he says, "like a miracle."

Bit by bit some of the poems began to reflect the newly won political insights which seemed so precious to some of the poets, especially the younger ones. They knew firsthand about being poor, about the depredations of Somoza, and about the work throughout Nicaragua being done by the Sandinista Front to prepare for an insurrection. Some of them, like Donald Guevara and Felipe Peña, had been using the meetings of the Grupo Jovenil (youth group) to raise the political consciousness of the young people in the islands. Angry poems began to be written: about poverty, about malnourished, uneducated kids, about the exploitation of the *campesinos* by large private companies, about the brutality of Somoza's Guardia Nacional. For instance, Elvis captures in only a few words an incident he's just heard about:

> They carried the wounded campesino
> down to his farm.
> Guardsmen had worked him over.
> Down from the thick mountains.
> Dying, dying.
> The wind ceaselessly moving the bushes.
> There on the far horizon
> the sun dropped out of sight.

Or Felipe Peña sees

> In the park at Granada
> fifteen old men with faces sad,

clothes dirty, shoes ripped,
glancing at one another.

Or Gloria Guevara, in "Misery," writes:

I came to a place
where they throw out
the whole town's garbage.

And I saw some kids
with some old sacks
they were filling with rusty cans
worn-out shoes
pieces of old cardboard box.

And some flies got into the sacks
and then they got out again
and settled down on the heads of the children.

Some even wrote poems imagining the kind of world they might have if the revolution ever came, a world of schools, decent food for everybody, healthy children, and no Guardia. "Before Ernesto came," Nubia Arcia told me, "before Mayra, before the poetry and the painting, our lives were *asleep*. That's what *campesino* life had always been—*una vida dormida*. They helped wake us up."

Mayra Jimenez was in Solentiname for only a couple of months. Things were changing quickly in Nicaragua, and Cardenal told her privately that the insurrection was nearing its flash point. He himself had already decided in the mid-70s that Ghandian nonviolence was impossible in Somoza's Nicaragua. He had joined the FSLN (Sandinista Liberation Front). "I became politicized by the contemplative life. Meditation is what brought me to political radicalization. I came to the revolution by way of the Gospels. It was not by reading Marx but Christ," he had written the previous year. Neutrality was no longer an option. Perhaps not even their "little paradise" in the lake would escape the consequences of armed struggle. He could not guarantee their safety. She and Antidio left Solentiname for Costa Rica.

5.

Partly through the experience of analyzing the Gospel and debating the nature of poetry, and partly through watching Ernesto himself evolve politically, the young peasant poets of Solentiname had reached a stage of radical Christianity, historical self-awareness, communal self-confidence and individual courage that made them ready to move beyond the interpretation, and even the production, of mere words. They felt the time had come for action to remove the evils they had witnessed and written about, and to take the first steps toward building the better world they had dreamed about and discussed. The FSLN had planned a series of attacks in different parts of Nicaragua for October 13, 1977. The rebels of the southernmost area had as their objective an assault on the garrison of the Guardia Nacional up on the hilltop that overlooks the town of San Carlos, the mouths of the Rio Frio and Rio San Juan, and out in the distance there in the lake, the islands of Solentiname.

The volunteers from Solentiname included Felipe Peña; Elvis Chavarría; Donald, Myriam, Alejandro, Julio Ramón, Gloria, and Iván Guevara; Nubia Arcia; Pedro Pablo Meneses; Bosco Centeno; Jose Arana; and Laureano Mairena. The training period was short. They learned from members of the Front how to disassemble, re-assemble, and fire the motley collection of weapons they had managed to collect: an old Garand, one M-1, one M-3 submachine gun, an old .45, a .22, an ancient 12-gauge shotgun. For some, it was the first time they had ever fired a gun.

As the 13th approached it was decided that most of the noncombatants—mainly older folks and children—should be sent to temporary safety in Costa Rica. Farewells were said. Felipe simply told old Tomás he'd be back in a week or so. Their parting is memorialized in his poem "Saying Goodbye to Father."

I said goodbye to you
Monday October 10th
You were sick, downcast.
You just sat there looking at me.
I promised I'd come back soon.
You squinted suspiciously
as though to say: You won't be back.

Your face sad
and you sitting on the old stool
you threw an arm around me and without speaking a word
resigned yourself to our farewell.
Embracing you for the last time I smiled
but my heart wept.
Only I knew where I was going
and why I was leaving you.

The Agudelos and Ernesto had already gone to Costa Rica; in fact, Ernesto was about to leave on one of his marathon speaking tours to different countries to drum up support for the FSLN.

The Solentiname rebels made their way to the mainland a few at a time so as not to arouse suspicion. Nubia recalls: "Iván and Pedro had to go first because they had some preliminary work to do. Then Gloria, Myriam and Felipe. That left only Elvis, Donald and me. We left the Community on the eve of the battle in the *San Juan de la Cruz*." The groups made their way either to safe houses in San Carlos or to farms in the vicinity. At one such farm, "La Loma," they made contact with "Zero" and "One," who would command the attack and who had some other guns, including a Browning Automatic Rifle, and ammunition. During the night the "La Loma" group set out for San Carlos, but their guide on horseback, an old man named "Carballito," got lost and they spent hours slogging around in the dark through swamps and thickets. But by dawn everyone was in place in San Carlos and armed. There were almost 20 of them by now.

At first light the order was given to open fire at the garrison for 10 minutes, after which the Guardia would be asked to surrender. "The fact is," says Julio Ramón, "it was never our intention to kill the guardsmen—they were just illiterates, it wasn't their fault, the blame belonged to their commanders, the big shots, the officials." But the Guardia refused to surrender, so the rebels opened fire again. Iván managed to toss a grenade into the kitchen, which was full of guardsmen. As he was running from house to house he came face to face with an old woman who began to scream, "Ayi! Here come the Sandinista guerrillas!" Some of the people were terrified, but others "lifted clenched fists as a sign of support." They began to move closer and closer, up the hill, over positions the Guardia had held. At one point Bosco turned: "There was Myriam, kneeling, her gun held in a better position than any of the rest of us. At her feet was a dead guardsman."

Ernesto "Chato" Medrano had been severely wounded while trying to throw a grenade. He was in the open. The others could see the great stain of blood spreading over his pants. Shouting that they should hold their positions, he somehow managed to crawl to cover. They could hear planes and helicopters. But they fought on. Nubia got on the radio to check about the other uprisings that were supposedly taking place all over Nicaragua at this moment—in Ocotal, Granada, Chinandega and elsewhere. But nothing had happened in those places. This meant that maybe the whole wrath of Somoza would be aimed at the San Carlos insurgents. But now the word came that the Guardia had fled the garrison by the back way and were heading toward the airport.

The kids from Solentiname had taken the garrison, if only temporarily. Alejandro was ready to burn the place down, but he heard the moans of wounded guardsmen inside and decided not to fry them alive. (This act of mercy, which preserved the main building, was later used by a Somoza spokesman as "proof" that the rebels had in fact not taken the garrison.) The fighting had lasted three hours. But there was no time to rest. "Zero" had been wounded and taken away. The Guardia would soon counterattack, this time with help from the air force. Among the other miscalculations for which he was later blamed, "Zero" had apparently not thought to arrange the means for a retreat. There was a frantic search for boats. They finally found a couple and headed up the Rio Frio toward Costa Rica. "Chato" was clearly dying and had to be left behind. Felipe Peña and Roberto Pichardo stayed in position to cover the others' retreat. Felipe's shotgun had jammed, he was surrounded, they told him to surrender. "OK, I surrender, just don't kill me, you sons of bitches!"

Helicopters had begun to chase them, so the rebels decided to ditch the boats and go on foot through the swamps. All night they trudged on. The mosquitos were voracious, clouds of them. There were snakes. They kept having to wade across the river as it looped back and forth. During one crossing Nubia slipped into deep water and began to drown. She called out to Iván, a strong swimmer, who was nearby in the darkness. But the first arm she felt around her was Alejandro's. (They would be married in Costa Rica on November 13th, a month to the day after the San Carlos assault.)

Next day they heard helicopters and were sure they'd been discovered, but no, they were passing close to "La Esperanza," a hacienda owned by Somoza, which the Guardia was using as a staging area. This meant they were not far from the border. Alejandro and "Chacal" stayed behind to cover the retreat and the rest headed south, keeping out of sight. After a while, says Gloria, "we heard the sound of a boat and some machine gun fire and we thought they'd killed our two guys. Only later did we learn that the shots we'd heard had been fired [by the Guardia] at Charpentier, the Costa Rican Minister of Security."

They walked and walked. Nubia had lost her shoes; her feet were cut and swollen. They were hungry and tired but afraid to stop at farms to ask for food in case they might still be in Nicaragua and guardsmen might be lying in wait for them. It was clear they were being followed. Once they were almost surrounded, but managed to slip away. Finally, after several days and nights of walking, they saw the lights of Los Chiles. They were only a few hundred yards from Costa Rica, where they would be granted asylum.

6.

The Guardia meanwhile had been busy. They had captured Jose Arana on Solentiname, beaten him up, and then proceeded to burn down every building in the Community—the library, the open hut where Gospel discussions had been held, the homes of Ernesto, the Agudelos, and the others—everything except the church, which they would use for a barracks. Elvis and Donald had been captured, beaten, and tied up. They were put on a boat in San Carlos and taken away (no one knew where). The last anyone saw of them, as the boat grew smaller, one of the two managed to raise a hand and make the "V" sign.

Felipe had been taken to La Bartolina Prison in San Carlos. He was stripped, tied up, beaten, interrogated, patched up, beaten again, starved, threatened again and again, but he never gave them the slightest sign that he'd been broken. After a week he was interviewed by reporters. He admitted belonging to the Sandinista Front. The reporters asked if he'd been paid. "I told them I was paid nothing because those who fight for the Front don't do it for pay, they do it because they want to." The colonel who ran the prison gave him a dirty look. Felipe was sure they'd try to find a pretext to kill him. He was finally brought before a judge and began to give a true account of who he was and what had happened and why he was fighting, but the judge was clearly writing down a different version. When Felipe protested, he was told, "It doesn't matter, we're going to shoot you anyway." "I don't care if you shoot me," Felipe told the judge. "Just write down what it was I said."

For several months the threats, interrogations, beatings and other abuses continued. A bare light bulb burned all night above his head, clouded with flying insects. Then in the early months of 1978 things got marginally better. The colonel allowed some women from San Carlos to visit Felipe. The colonel told him Somoza had lifted his death sentence, and that the Red Cross was going to visit the prison. Suddenly things got almost comically better: the prisoners got heavy doses of malaria pills; they were told they might be released; they were given the supplies needed to clean up the entire filthy prison, whitewash the walls, and fill up the stinking pit swimming with human waste, maggots and garbage; they were each given a cot and pillow (they'd been sleeping on the bare concrete floors up to that point), fresh clothes, magazines, and finally even a radio. When the Red Cross man asked, he was told by the prison officials that all these amenities had always been there. Most of the prisoners, fearing reprisals, corroborated the story. But not Felipe.

After about six months he heard a woman asking one of the guards what had happened to Elvis Chavarría and Donald Guevara. "Oh, we killed them," was the reply. Felipe couldn't tell if the guard was joking or telling the truth, but he feared the worst. In fact, Elvis and Donald had been taken not, as some thought, to a prison in Managua, but to the hacienda "La Esperanza." With hands tied together behind their backs they had been tortured, questioned, and then shot in the head and buried. Their bodies were not found until after the triumph of the revolution two years later. The cords used to bind their wrists have been preserved and can be seen in the restored library in Solentiname— the two larger loops for Elvis, the smaller ones for Donald.

Finally on August 20, 1978, a Sandinista commando group led by Eden Pastora stormed the National Palace in Managua and took some members of the National Assembly hostage. The rebels demanded $10 million, the release of all political prisoners, and free passage to Panama. Somoza reluctantly agreed. Three days later an incredulous Felipe Peña, along with other political prisoners, was taken out the front gate of La Bartolina. In the park across the way were maybe 400 people from San Carlos and Solentiname cheering and waving goodbye with their handkerchiefs. (Felipe has captured this moment in "The Day of My Release.") Then a flight to Managua, transfer to the central police station, the arrival of other prisoners from elsewhere in the country, and finally the triumphant bus ride through the capital toward the airport, the streets jammed with thousands of Nicaraguans shouting, "Long live the FSLN! Long live National Liberation!" The plane flew them to Panama. Within months Felipe Peña was back in Nicaragua (via Costa Rica, where he had a reunion with Mayra Jimenez and other poets from Solentiname), this time in a real uniform, well armed, fighting against Somoza. Shortly before the final victory he was killed in a battle near Nueva Guinea.

7.

From an artistic point of view, the assault on San Carlos and the subsequent exile in Costa Rica of most of the poets was an important turning point in the maturing of poetic voices. The poems written in exile (or back "in the mountains" of Nicaragua while fighting for the revolution) show a sharp qualitative jump over the earlier exercises. The post-assault poems of Felipe, Bosco, Iván, Gloria, Pedro, Nubia and doña Olivia tend to be longer, richer in detail, more confident and thoughtful than before; they simply have more *meat* to them. If literacy can bring with it the sort of critical consciousness of your relationship to the world that can lead to both self-expression and meaningful political action, then the aftermath of an act of open rebellion can be a time in which your new self grows every day more sinewy and agile—in a word, more empowered—in both language and action. The poems written by the Solentiname poets after the San Carlos assault exhibit not only new subject matter, but also breakthroughs in form and method.

Felipe Peña, for instance, writes after the attack two of his longest poems. "Seven-Thirty" has as its frame a chance meeting with a girl he had last seen two years earlier, in May of 1977, but at its core is a carefully wrought series of memories about a trip to see the girl, meeting up with Elvis and Donald, his capture by the Guardia, his prison days, and finally his release followed by seeing the girl again. No previous poem of his has this amount of detail and narrative force. The same is true of "A Good Leader," which draws us into the life of a *guerrillero* as a way of paying tribute to his commanding officer, the Spanish priest Gaspar García Laviana (although it is only after Gaspar's death that Felipe learns he was a priest.) This new urge of Felipe's to work through complex experiences in the body of a single poem was made clear to Mayra Jimenez the last time she saw him, in Costa Rica. He was feverish and exhausted from his prison experience, but he told her one morning, "I've been trying these days to write a long poem I've got in my head; but I've got to give it form, coordinate the ideas." When she came back to see him that afternoon, she learned that he'd been called back into action in Nicaragua. The last time anyone saw him was near Nueva Guinea. He was kneeling by a badly wounded *compañero*, refusing to leave him there to die. The Guardia was closing in. Felipe's body was never found. That last poem was never written down. Or perhaps we could say the poem was *enacted* rather than written.

Bosco Centeno is clearly the poet who matured most between October of 1977 and the publication of the anthology *Poesia Campesina de Solentiname* in 1980. In "This Moon Half-Hidden" his disgust with life in exile, especially the noisy urban setting of San Jose, is matched by a powerful nostalgia for home, for the sweet natural world of Solentiname. This of course is a theme many of the exiled poets will echo. But Bosco's verse has begun to tighten up. Witness for instance the striking imagery of "Just as a Tapir" in which that bizarre Central American animal is pictured wrenching itself free from a jaguar but leaving behind, imbedded in the attacker, some of its (the tapir's) sharp claws. And then the twist:

> so I ripped the memory of you
> trembling like a startled doe
> out of my mind
> though it was you
> who carried away
> some part of me.

Bosco's war poems are also brisk and clear-eyed: "Hiding Ourselves in the Night," "Sweaty and Muddy," and "Brother Guardsman, Forgive Me." But the real leap forward is in his long visionary poem "Solentiname," in which the entire experience of the Community on Mancarrón is recapitulated—from the innocence of girls, fishing, fiestas, Gospel discussions, through the San Carlos assault and the image of Donald and Elvis "captured, their heads bloodied, trussed up like burlap sacks in the launch" that would take them to their deaths—followed by a radiant vision of the future of Solentiname in which the best of the past will be fused with a new reality. And finally there is the poem to his friend Tony ("Chicha") who fell in combat near Nueva Guinea, and who always kept a kernel of corn in his shirt pocket. In an archetypal Central American image, the poet imagines that the blood of the fallen warrior irrigated the kernel, which sprouted "and grew into huge and mighty stalks." Bosco is breaking new ground in these poems.

The other poets, writing in a workshop-in-exile convened by Mayra and Ernesto, also expand on their new-found themes: memories of combat and flight; the bitterness of exile; separation from loved ones; longing for Solentiname, imagining how quiet and desolate the destroyed Community must be; political anger and resolution. But of course there are personal variations on these themes.

Gloria writes the first dream-poem of the group, "Last Night I Dreamt," a tense mix of fact and fantasy. Iván rises into pure elegy, imagining the place he grew up now ruined and abandoned ("In Solentiname," "The Deserted Church"). He also writes the bitterly ironic "You Can Hear Speeches Like This," about the gap between language and deeds, and a couple of the best long poems in the collection, "Four Days in the Mountains, Then Exile," and "From a Hilltop on the Benjamin Zeledón Southern Front." Pedro Pablo seems incurably lonely and homesick, imagining the minute details of nature even in the midst of war. Nubia's "Letter" is a masterful fusion of elements: her daughter playing on the bed, the photo of Sandino, the hollowed out hand grenade with a flower stuck in the top, and the letter from Alejandro to the Agudelos (they have passed it on to her) in which he describes his secret position in the mountains, from which he can see Solentiname. Myriam, in "To Chato Medrano," gives us the best picture of the assault itself. And Myriam's "After the Battle," Elena Pineda's "When the Kids from Solentiname . . ." and Olivia Silva's "During the Assault" give us vivid pictures of what the members of the Community went through on their way to exile. Doña Olivia, matriarch of the Guevara clan, expands on her strongest themes: the suffering of children (both her own and those of other mothers), food, memories of better days, and a deep hatred of *somocismo*. Eddy Chavarría, Elvis's younger brother, seems even more lonely and bitter than Pedro Pablo; his strong quiet poems from exile sound the only notes of real desperation in the collection.

As for Elvis, with his spare, rhythmic, minimalist, gemlike verses, and Donald, with his powerful descriptive gifts (in "Cattle," for instance), how might they have developed as poets had they survived the assault? Those who have asked similar questions about Keats and Chatterton, or about Lorca and the Salvadoran poet Roque Dalton, know the vanity of such speculations. We are lucky to have the handful of poems we do.

8.

In July of 1979 the revolution triumphed. "When the war ended," Ernesto has told Margaret Randall, "I thought I would be able to go back to live on the island. After all those years of struggle, so much traveling and exile, underground and agitation, I dreamed of returning to Solentiname, rebuilding the community and writing the chronicle of this revolution. But the revolution had other plans for me.

"It was Father D'Escoto who called me in Costa Rica to ask if I'd accept a cabinet post as Minister of Culture. I said I didn't much like the idea, but if that was an order, I'd accept. He asked me again, 'Do you accept?' and again I said if it was an order I'd have to. 'But do you accept?' he insisted. And I finally said, 'Yes.' "

One of Ernesto's first acts as Minister of Culture was to call on Mayra Jimenez to help plan poetry workshops for all of Free Nicaragua. These workshops have been a great success, redefining the meaning of literacy in Nicaragua, and exposing soldiers, nurses, factory workers, carpenters, students, fishermen, domestic employees, mechanics and many others to the world of reading and writing poetry, and to the rigors and rewards of the workshop setting in which writing is shared and criticized openly and honestly. The exigencies of war which have weakened the transportation system in Nicaragua have made the functioning of some of these workshops extremely difficult. And there have been charges that the workshops produce canned, mechanical, hollow political verse rather than real poetry. But an objective observer would find that enough good, original work has emerged, and enough people have made the workshops a regular weekly part of their lives, to justify the program.

Another early step by the Ministry of Culture was the publication in 1980 of *Poesia Campesina de Solentiname*, representing the fruits of the first of Nicaragua's poetry workshops. The anthology has been widely published in the Spanish-speaking world and elsewhere.

As for the Solentiname poets who survived the insurrection and the war that followed, the picture is fragmented. In 1987 only two continue to write and publish poetry: Bosco Centeno and Iván Guevara, both of whom are officers in the army, where poetry workshops are still regularly held. Bosco's Solentiname work plus a number of newer poems have been published as *Puyonearon los granos* (The Kernels Sprouted), which won the Leonel Rugama Younger Poets Prize in 1981.

There is no longer a poetry workshop in Solentiname. Many of the original poets are scattered or are doing other things. A number of those who worked in both poetry and painting in the '70s have chosen to concentrate solely on painting, for which the Ministry of Culture has cultivated a wide market. Gloria works for the government and still paints. She and her sister Myriam (also a painter) and their mother, doña Olivia Silva (also a painter) live most of the time in Managua. Doña Olivia has been trying to lead painting workshops in the prisons of Managua. It's hard going, she says: "They haven't got the innate patience with detail that's required." Her son William is studying in Cuba; Esperanza, a painter, is married to Bosco Centeno. Elena Pineda, the widow of Laureano Mairena, lives in Managua. Of the original adult poets, only Nubia Arcia (wife of Alejandro Guevara, the governor of the Rio San Juan region and a member of the National Assembly) and Elvis's mother doña Natalia Sequeira, live in Solentiname. Nubia paints, raises her children, and is manager of a new woodworking cooperative on the biggest island, where islanders use state-of-the-art (donated) West German machines to turn out a line of furniture and all-wooden toys. Doña Natalia still lives in the simple house where Elvis was born and raised, along with her daughter, the painter Milagros Chavarría. Next door is the one-room Elvis Chavarría School. The old woman suffers from headaches and other unspecified complaints that began when Elvis first left home to take part in the assault on San Carlos. She no longer writes much, preferring to spend her time rocking, staring out over the lake past the Guevara homestead to the mountains of Costa Rica. Unlike doña Olivia, who also lost a son in the insurrection but knows what the sacrifice meant, doña Natalia seems bitter and confused about politics.

Pedro Pablo Meneses deserted the Sandinista cause in the early '80s and went to join forces with Eden Pastora's ARDE in Costa Rica. But he never actually fought against his old *compañeros* from Solentiname. He was killed in suspicious circumstances shortly after he made contact with Pastora's group. Rumor in Solentiname has it that ARDE thought he was a Sandinista spy, which of course he wasn't. But, continues the conventional wisdom, "he was never very sophisticated politically. He should have known they might suspect him."

One of the few members of the Guevara family not a member of the original poetry workshop is Mariita, one of the best Solentiname painters, who along with her husband Juan Alarníz operates the archipelago's only hotel. She remembers the three poets who died. "My brother Donald was a great worker. He really got things done! Sometimes he'd work well into the night. He and Elvis and Felipe, they did everything: fishing, farming, construction. And transport, that was Donald's specialty. If somebody was sick, say, and it was the middle of the night and they had to take the person to the doctor in San Carlos, Donald was the person they could always depend on. . . . He was very calm, always had a lot of tact. And he was a great dreamer, always dreaming about the future.

"Felipe was a great worker, too. Very strong. And always happy, very friendly, especially with the women. A very sweet, very brotherly guy, the happiest of the lot. Like Elvis, he played guitar, sang a lot. He even composed some songs. In the Gospel discussions, whenever he spoke his opinions were always strongly held, sure of himself, always positive.

"Elvis was the calmest, the most patient. He loved to play with children. They all loved him. He played the guitar. He was just . . . calm in his mind.

"The three of them were really progressive. Everyone around here thought of them as natural leaders."

Things are pretty quiet in Solentiname these days, although with the new woodworking factory starting up and the double row of handsome new houses near it financed by donations from an Italian labor union, things are looking up. But there has been a change in geographic nomenclature: the three largest islands have new names. Isla Venada is now called Isla Donald Guevara. Isla San Fernando is now called Isla Elvis Chavarría. And Isla Mancarrón is now called Isla Felipe Peña.

—David Gullette

22

Nicaraguan Peasant Poetry
from Solentiname

FELIPE PEÑA

FROM MY WINDOW

Way over there on another island I see
the house of doña Francisca
(Lurio's mother-in-law,
Blanca's mama)
who almost every Saturday makes pork tamales;
and of don Santos, who sells us that White Rum
whenever we drop by for supper.

MARINA

Marina
I came by your house by pure chance
and you made me feel right at home
I had supper and I felt good there
and I know you won't say
what Myriam says
that I'm like some hound dog howling at the moon
just so I'll cross from one island
to another.

LUCRECIA [1]

Lucrecia: I dreamt your mama
invited me to your house
and all I saw were the faces of strangers.
And if, now I'm awake, I went to your house
I still wouldn't see you because you're not there.
In any case, I decided some time ago not to see you
(even though, when I woke up, I wanted to see you).

DESDE MI VENTANA

Lejos en otra isla veo
la casa de doña Francisca
la suegra de Lurio
la mamá de la Blanca,
la que hace nacatamales casi todo los sábados;
y don Santos, que nos vende el "Ron Plata"
cuando llegamos a cenar.

MARINA

Marina
a tu casa llegué por pura coincidencia
y me recibiste bien
cené y estuve contento
y vos no me dirás
como la Myriam
que parezco perro aullando
para que me vaya a cruzar de una isla a otra.

LUCRECIA

Lucrecia: soñé que tu mamá
me invitó a tu casa,
y sólo caras extrañas vi.
Y si ahora que estoy despierto voy,
tampoco te vería porque no estás;
de todos modos hace tiempo decidí no verte
aunque cuando me desperté quería.

LUCRECIA [2]

Lucrecia, I will no longer drop by your house
no longer come calling in motorboat or rowboat
no longer wake up your pa at midnight
no longer splash down the muddy roads of Pueblo Nuevo.
And no longer will you make up the cot with a pillow and bedspread.

I SAW YOU

I saw you gazing down the road
I was coming down — Oh, did that make me feel happy!
And I was about to whistle to you
so you'd wait for me
when I saw a man in a red cap,
sitting at the foot of the guacimón tree
who called out to you. Later
your brother told me
that's where you went
to meet your sweetheart.

I'M SO PROUD OF THE PLACE I WAS BORN

I'm so proud of the place I was born
and I love it even more when I remember my childhood,
the madroño trees in full flower
that adorned the hilltops of our islands.
But I grow sad when I think of Santiago
who can't find work
who plants but doesn't harvest
and of his wife Pablita
who scrounges around but comes up empty.
The kids are like corpses.
But I feel better when I hear
the toads the frogs the doves sing.
These are our jukeboxes.

LUCRECIA

Lucrecia, ya no llegaré a tu casa
ya no viajaré en bote de remo ni de motor
ya no despertaré a tu papá a media noche
ya no pasaré los caminos de Pueblo Nuevo chapoteando lodo
ya no vas a tender la tijera con la almohada y la colcha.

TE VI

Te vi mirando hacia el camino
por el que iba yo. ¡Qué alegría sentí!
Ya te iba a silbar para que me esperaras,
y miré a un hombre, gorra roja,
sentado en las gambas de un guacimón,
que te llamó. Después tu hermano me dijo
que allí recibías la visita de tu enamorado.

ME ENORGULLECE EL SITIO EN QUE NACÍ

Me enorgullece el sitio en que nací
y me enamoro más cuando recuerdo me infancia
los árboles de madroño florecido
que adornaban la montaña de nuestras islas.
Pero me entristezco cuando pienso en Santiago
que no encuentra trabajo
que siembra y no cosecha,
en su mujer la Pablita
que busca donde no hay.
Los niños parecen cadáveres.
Pero me distraigo cuando oigo cantar los sapos
las ranas las palomas.
Estas son las roconolas nuestras.

THE GIRLS

I'd given up waiting for them.
Night fell and things had come to a turning point.
Half hour later, everything was dazzling
like when a cloud blots the brightness of the moon
then passes.

IN THE BOAT

Way over there in the haze
straight ahead, where that boat is heading
is Colón. And on the other side,
Point Pizote.
In between, you can see the sandbar
where my pa used to set up camp
whenever we came to fish.
You can't see the ceiba tree
where the guás would perch and sing.
And way beyond, all you can see is a zinc house
glowing in the sun.

TO MY FATHER

Every time I come to see you I get depressed.
I really miss your advice, the stories
you used to tell about your friends, the women you knew.
I never hear you laugh anymore.
I can tell from these gestures you make you're fairly content;
you struggle to make signs with the one good hand you have left.
And when I don't understand, you turn serious
your eyes drop
and they're ringed with tears.

LAS MUCHACHAS

Ya no las esperaba.
Anocheció y todo era crítico.
Media hora después todo espléndido
como cuando una nube tapa la claridad de la luna
y pasa.

YENDO EN BOTE

Alla en aquello humoso,
recto, adonde el bote va,
está Colón. A la par está
la Punta de Pizote.
En medio se ve el banco de arena
donde mi papá se ranchaba cuando veníamos a pescar.
No se ve el palo de ceiba donde se paraba el guás a cantar.
Allí sólo se ve una casa de zinc,
que relumbra con el sol.

A MI PADRE

Cada vez que te vengo a ver me entristezco.
Me hacen falta tus consejos, las anécdotas
que me platicabas de tus amigos o tuyas.
Ya no te escucho reír alegre.
Sé que estás contento por el gesto que hacés;
te afanás haciendo señas con la mano que te ha quedado buena.
Y cuando no te entiendo, te ponés serio,
mirás para abajo,
y se te rodean los ojos de lágrimas.

THE MOON SHINES AS THOUGH IT WERE DAY

The moon shines as though it were day
and I remember the time I slept
in that house alone
amid the cold pricking of the mosquitos
wishing the night were minutes.
And you, Lucrecia,
you were probably laughing
or something
who knows?

IT'S BEEN RAINING ALL DAY

It's been raining all day.
It's already three in the afternoon.
The guys are cutting wood: pow, pow, pow.
The little birds are sad: chiu, chiu, chiu.
The wind has died down.
Along the shoreline the water is choppy.
The narrow channels have filled up.
Sardines, choppers, and barbudos
crowd upstream to spawn
and where they are thickest
the herons, puncos, and guairones gather.

IN THE PARK AT GRANADA

In the park at Granada
15 old men with faces sad,
clothes dirty, shoes ripped,
glancing at one another.

LA LUNA ALUMBRA COMO SI FUERA EL DÍA

La luna alumbra como si fuera el día
y recuerdo la vez que dormí en
aquella casa solo
con frío picado de zancudos
queriendo que la noche fuera minutos.
Y vos Lucrecia
te estarías riendo
o quién sabe.

TODO EL DÍA HA PASADO LLOVIENDO

Todo el día ha pasado lloviendo.
Ya son las 3 de la tarde.
Los muchachos cortan leña,
se oye el golpe del hacha: pon, pon, pon.
Los pajaritos están tristes: chui, chui, chui.
El viento se quedó calmo.
En la costa el agua está revuelta.
Las quebradas están llenas.
Las sardinas, los dientones y los barbudos
trepan en las correntadas a desovar,
y donde hay más, se reúnen
las garzas, los puncos y los guairones.

EN EL PARQUE DE GRANADA

En el parque de Granada
quince viejos con la cara triste,
la ropa sucia, los zapatos rotos,
viéndose unos a otros.

PLAGUES

Plagues can be natural or artificial.
In Solentiname the plagues include
parrots, agoutis, zanates, mice,
army ants, not to mention moths,
not to mention the merchants who devour the campesinos' harvest,
and of course the bosses who devour the labor of the farmhands
just as parrots, agoutis, zanates,
mice, and army ants eat up your corn and rice and beans.
Well, these human plagues are part of a System of Plagues.
Here in Solentiname the Company has managed to
eliminate the parrots, mice, and agoutis
which are among the plagues that screw the campesinos
so I figure the company will just have to
eliminate the human plague, too
and when I say company
I don't mean the Railroad Company,
I mean the company of workers.

SAYING GOODBYE TO FATHER

I said goodbye to you
Monday October 10th.
You were sick, downcast.
You just sat there looking at me.
I promised I'd come back soon.
You squinted suspiciously
as though to say: You won't be back.
Your face sad
and you sitting on the old stool
you threw an arm around me and without speaking a word
resigned yourself to our farewell.
Embracing you for the last time I smiled
but my heart wept.
Only I knew where I was going
and why I was leaving you.

PLAGAS

Las plagas pueden ser naturales o artificiales.
En Solentiname las plagas son
los loros, guatuzas, los zanates, ratones;
zompopos, también hay polillas
como también hay comerciantes que devoran las cosechas
de los campesinos,
como también patrones que devoran el trabajo de los peones,
igual que los loros, guatuzas, zanates,
ratones, zompopos, devoran el maíz, el arroz, los frijoles.
También las plagas humanas constituyen un sistema de plagas.
Aquí en Solentiname la Compañía ha hecho desaparecer los loros,
los ratones, las guatuzas,
que son parte de las plagas que joden al campesino
y creo que la compañía hará desaparecer
la plaga humana, claro que no la Compañía del Tránsito
sino la del proletariado.

DESPEDIDA DEL PADRE

Me despedí de vos
el lunes 10 de octubre.
Estabas enfermo con la mirada baja.
Me quedaste viendo.
Te prometí volver pronto.
Entrecerraste tus ojos maliciosamente
queriendo decirme: vos no volvés.
Tu cara triste
sentado en el viejo taburete
me echaste el brazo y sin pronunciar palabra
te resignaste a decirme adiós.
Abrazándote por última vez me sonreía
pero mi corazón lloraba.
Sólo yo sabía hacia dónde iba
y por qué te dejaba.

YOU THINK

You think I'm not in love
and that I'm a jerk because I pretend not to understand
what's hidden in your words, your tone of voice,
          the sly looks you send my way.
Maybe — seeing how little I seem to care —
you doubt your own beauty.
I don't want you to picture me this way.
Please, think it through, imagine:
What can a guerrillero offer you,
and he slogging through mud on mountain roads,
sleeping on a mat of slashed branches
or on the ground, wrapped in plastic?
What can I offer you if I've offered my life to the people?
What do I have
except my knapsack, my gun, my ration of ammo,
and my uniform of olive drab?

VISIT FROM A GIRL

Yesterday you came by surprise
You sat down and looked into the cell
I never imagined you'd come to see me
You didn't care how much the guards humiliated you.
And today, you didn't care about the rain
You promised you'd come and you came.
Everything I may suffer in prison
I'll forget —
But your looks, your words, your farewell kiss
I will never forget, Cristina.

VOS CREÉS

Vos creés que yo no me enamoro
y pensás que soy pendejo porque me hago el que no entiendo
el contenido de tus palabras, el acento de tu voz, la malicia
    de tus miradas.
Posiblemente dudás de tu belleza, por la poca importancia
    que aparento darle,
no quisiera pensar que tenés esa imagen de mí,
te pido que reflexionés y que pensés qué puede
ofrecerte un guerrillero que anda chapoteando lodo
en los caminos de la montaña, durmiendo en tapescos de varas,
o envuelto en un plástico en el suelo. Qué puedo ofrecerte yo
si mi vida se la he ofrecido al pueblo,
no tengo más que la mochila, el fusil, la dotación de tiros
y mi uniforme de verde olivo.

VISITA DE UNA AMIGA

Ayer viniste sorpresivamente
te sentaste viendo para la celda
nunca imaginé que vinieras a verme
sin importarte la humillación que te hicieron los guardias.
Hoy no te importó la lluvia
prometiste que venías y viniste.
Todo lo que sufra en la cárcel se me olvidará
pero tus miradas tus palabras
y el beso de despedida no lo olvidaré Cristina.

THE SOMOZA REVIEW

I'm sitting on the cement floor of La Bartolina
and the guard slips us this magazine
with a picture of Old Somoza and his sons —
the one who had the General of Free Men killed
and the one who's killing our people now.
I look at Somoza Debayle mounted on his Peruvian horse . . .
       I tried to read, but what I saw grew dark:
       Instead of letters, black stains.

PRISON VISITS

Mother Mara, after your visit I no longer went unnoticed.
You broke the silence I'd been stuck in at San Carlos
ever since my capture. Esterlina felt encouraged to come, and
Consuelo de Pilarte and Cristina María,
who later celebrated her birthday one Sunday with
those of us who'd been captured,
the girl with black eyes sparkling
like piercing bright-eyed stars, like a ray of light,
and those others who came to see me on Sundays
and the ladies who came with the girls
who gave us cool drinks when the guards took us out to work.

NOSTALGIA FROM PRISON

After four months of not seeing the sun
for the first time at two in the afternoon the head guard
opened the lock of La Bartolina: "Felipe,
you're gonna cut some wood." I stepped outside.
Like a fox looking out of his hole in all directions
I stood there hopeless, staring out over the beach
at the blue outline of the isles of Solentiname
and the long boats fading slowly away toward Granada
and for a moment I dreamt that one day
I too would be sailing toward my beloved islands
or toward Granada.

LA REVISTA DE SOMOZA

Estoy sentado en el piso de cemento de La Bartolina
y el guardia nos pasa con cautela la revista
en la que aparecen Somoza viejo y sus hijos
el que hizo asesinar al General de Hombres Libres
y el que asesina a nuestro pueblo actualmente.
Miro a Somoza Debayle montado en un caballo peruano
quise leer pero se me oscureció la vista
las letras las vi como manchas negras.

LAS VISITAS A LA CÁRCEL

Hasta que viniste vos madre Mara dejé de estar inadvertido.
Rompiste el silencio que había en San Carlos
desde me captura. Se animó la Esterlina
la Consuelo de Pilarte la Cristina María
que después celebró su cumpleaños un domingo con los que
estábamos presos, la joven de ojos negros, relucientes
como luceros penetrantes como un rayo de luz
y las otras que llegaban a verme los domingos
y las señoras con las muchachas
que nos daban fresco cuando nos sacaban a trabajar.

NOSTALGIA DESDE LA CÁRCEL

Después de cuatro meses de no ver el sol,
por primera vez a las 2 de la tarde el cabo de guardia
abrio el candado de La Bartolina: Felipe, vas a picar leña, salí.
Como la zorra de su cueva viendo para todos lados
desesperado quedé viendo la playa al frente
las manchas azules son las islas de Solentiname
y las lanchas alejándose poco a poco rumbo a Granada
y me hice la ilusión de viajar un día
a mis islas amadas o a Granada.

THE DAY OF MY RELEASE

Today the 23d of August at eight-thirty in the morning
I saw the sun shining
I stopped smelling the stench of shit and piss
No more mosquito bites, no more sleeping on the concrete floor
Today I leave behind the flies and maggots in the pits of La Bartolina
No more bare lightbulbs shining in my eyes all night
and the gnats that kept me from sleeping
No longer will the lieutenant tell me I'm unpatriotic
and that I don't deserve even the air I breathe.
I leave behind the guards who tried to kill me
and even you I leave behind, you folks from my hometown,
with your hands lifted over there in the park
waving goodbye with your handkerchiefs.

IT'S FIVE-THIRTY

It's five-thirty in the afternoon, the weather is calm
no sound of the spotter plane that patrols the border
only the mumblemumble of some compañeros talking in their lean-to
and birdsongs from the mountain as the evening closes in —
the dove, the guás
the partridge that whistles like someone lost in the woods
the choschos
the howler monkeys chanting con con con
the woodpecker pecking a dead limb
and the monkeys having fun in the leafy trees
shrieking and throwing dry sticks.
This afternoon the crickets are all turned on
they sing ririri as though to announce the rain that starts to fall.
The mountain has clouded over, some of us are going to take up
          our posts,
others are going to sleep without their supper.

DÍA DE LA LIBERACIÓN

Hoy 23 de agosto a las 8 y media de la mañana
vi el sol reluciente
dejé de sentir tufo a mierda y a orines
ya no me picarán los zancudos ni dormiré en el piso de cemento
hoy se quedan las moscas y los gusanos en los hoyos de La Bartolina,
ya no estará encendida la luz en toda la noche
y los sayules [chayules] que no me dejaban dormir.
No me dirá el teniente que soy anti patria
y que no merezco ni el aire que respiro,
se quedan los guardias que me quisieron matar y vos
gente de mi pueblo te quedás
con las manos levantadas desde el parque
diciendo adiós con tus peñuelos.

SON LAS CINCO Y MEDIA

Son las 5 y media de la tarde, el tiempo está sereno
no se oye el sonido de la avioneta que vigila la frontera
sólo el gurún gurún de los compañeros que hablan desde sus champas
y el canto de los pájaros en la montaña al atardecer
la gongolona el guás
la perdiz que silba como persona perdida en los bosques
el choschós
los congos que cantan con con con
el pájaro carpintero picotea en un palo seco
y los monos que hacen gracias en los árboles frondosos
chillan y botan ramas secas.
Esta tarde más que las otras se han animado más los grillos
que cantan ri ri ri como si anunciaran la lluvia que empieza a caer
la montaña se ha oscuredico, nosotros vamos a hacer la posta
los otros a dormir sin haber cenado.

BLANCA I'M SAD

Blanca I'm sad
The sun doesn't shine this afternoon like yesterday
Your absence has left me in the grip of
        desperation, silence, melancholy.
Yesterday it was you who told me, horrified,
how Somoza's Guardia had killed your mother
and your brother William
only 15,
and how
where the bodies had been left
the vultures dove down and rose again
like planes that dive and rise again
bombing.

SEVEN-THIRTY

Seven-thirty at night I saw you.
Knowing I'd made no mistake, I headed toward you.
You were standing with three others at the edge of the park
opposite the hotel where I was staying.
I hadn't seen you since Thursday the 26th of May 1977
when I came from Granada to Solentiname and
said goodbye to you at two in the afternoon.
The look on your face seemed to beg a kiss
but I was naïve and gave you my hand when
you told me I should come to the Valley of Guadalupe
to your mother's house for the July vacation.
And I came: we almost sank crossing the lake from the islands
to the mouth of the Rio Papaturro.
It had been raining and the roads were muddy.
You weren't home.
They told me you'd gone to a dance.
Dónald, your cousin, and Elvis, your sister's boyfriend
also came with me and later Somoza's Guardia
murdered them when we made our attack on San Carlos
October 13th of that same year.

BLANCA ESTOY TRISTE

Blanca estoy triste.
Esta tarde no brilla el sol como el de ayer.
La ausencia de vos ha hecho que se apodere de mí
el desespero, el silencio y la melancolía.
Ayer eras vos quien horrorizada
me platicabas cómo los guardias somocistas
asesinaron a tu mamá y a tu hermano William
de quince años
y que los zopilotes allí donde dejaron
los cadáveres bajaban y subían
como aviones que bajan y suben
bombardeando.

A LAS SIETE Y MEDIA

A las siete y media de la noche te vi.
Sin temor a equivocarme me dirigí a vos.
Estabas parada con tres más a orillas del parque
frente al hotel donde me hospedé.
No te había visto desde el jueves 26 de mayo de 1977
cuando venía de Granada a Solentiname y
me despedí de vos a las dos de la tarde.
Con tu mirada me pedías un beso
pero ingenuamente te di la mano cuando
me decías que llegara al valle de Guadalupe
a la casa de tu mamá para las vacaciones del mes de julio.
Y llegué: casi nos hundimos cruzando el lago de las islas
a la bocana del río Papaturro.
Había estado lloviendo y los caminos estaban lodosos.
Vos no estabas en casa.
Me dijeron que andabas en un baile.
Dónald, tu primo, y Elvis el enamorado de tu hermana
también llegaron conmigo y después la guardia somocista
los asesinó cuando el ataque que hicimos en San Carlos
el trece de octubre de ese mismo año.

I was captured.
By some miracle of God the Guardia didn't kill me.
They were like mad dogs
when I surrendered with my shotgun
which had jammed on me.
Four months I was incommunicado,
deprived of even a friend's smile.
I thought I'd never see you again.
Then there were a couple of months when things got better:
the people of the village got to like me,
even the guards let us out to use the privy three times a day.
February, March, April it was like summer:
glory days in prison: I could see the sun, the shore
drying out, the isles of Solentiname,
and the boats that came from Granada every Tuesday
morning and began their return in the afternoon.
I remembered our innocent goodbye
and once again I dreamed of seeing you
the same way I saw freedom when I got out of prison.
And although after two years of not seeing you
it seems too good to be believed,
here I am, seeing you.

A GOOD LEADER

I met you at the beginning of September
in a column of 35 soldiers of the Army of the People.
You were doing rearguard with Compañera Marta and me.
Your alias was "Martín."
You and El Danto commanded the column
and he, an expert in trekking through the mountains of Nicaragua,
was point man, leading the march.
We'd been resting in the shade of a leafy tree
we'd come across while climbing one of the hills.
We were about to move on when El Danto shouted to me:
"Hide! The planes'll see you!"
His voice surprised me
I tried to run but fell.

42

Yo caí preso. Por milagro de Dios no me mataron los guardias
que parecían perros con rabia
cuando yo me rendí con mi escopeta
que se me enconchó.
Estuve cuatro meses incomunicado,
carecí hasta de la sonrisa de un amigo.
Pensé que no te volvería a ver.
Y vinieron dos meses más alivianados,
la gente del pueblo me admiraba,
hasta los guardias nos sacaban
tres veces al día al excusado.
Era verano entre febrero, marzo y abril:
días de gloria en la cárcel: podía ver el sol, las costas
que se estaban secando, las islas de Solentiname
y las lanchas que venían de Granada los martes en
la mañana y por la tarde se alejaban de regreso.
Yo recordaba la despedida ingenua
y nuevamente me hacía la ilusión de verte
como vi la libertad cuando salí de las cárceles.
Y después de dos años de no verte
aunque parece mentira
te estoy viendo.

UN BUEN DIRIGENTE

Te conocí a principios del mes de septiembre
en una columna de 35 soldados del ejército del pueblo
vos ibas en la retaguardia con la compañera Marta y yo.
Tu pseudonimo era Martín.
Vos y el Danto comandaban la columna
este último experto en caminatas en las montañas de Nicaragua
iba adelante dirigiendo la marcha.
Estuvimos sentados descansando debajo de la sombra de unos
        árboles frondosos
que encontramos al subir una de las lomas.
Íbamos llegando cuando me gritó el Danto:
escóndanse que los ven los aviones.
Me sorprendió su voz
intenté correr y me caí.

Another group of compañeros had made a hit on the command post
at Peñas Blancas that morning
and the air force was bombing.
We heard the rockets exploding
400 meters away.
The order came to advance.
I was all tangled up in a canebrake.
We came out into a clearing,
the brush hid us knee-deep,
and the planes went right overhead.
Angrily I shouted: "This is criminal!
They drag us out of the woods into a clearing!"
And you, Martín, shouted: "Take it easy!
When the plane comes by just drop where you are and sit still!"
Running, then freezing, we made it to a ravine.
There you took off your shoes and seeing how worried we were
said with absolute calm:
"If they drop a bomb we'll come back here;
but nobody's going to run."
We stayed there until four in the afternoon. At six
we approached a house you ordered us to take.
I got scared and timidly asked
"We're not going to . . . do anything to these people, are we?"
And you answered firmly: "NO."
You bought a pig and two chickens from them.
The night was rainy,
we lay down in shacks where hens were roosting.
Compañero Malicia was shaking with fever
and there were no blankets.
And the following night we came back,
having given up any chance of attacking the Rivas command post.
On the main road a guardsman arrested you,
and deported you to Panama,
but later I saw you again in camp
directing drill from five to six in the morning
and in the evening holding political discussions.

Otro grupo de compañeros había hecho un pequeño ataque al comando
de Peñas Blancas esa mañana
y la aviación estaba bombardeando.
Oíamos los rockets que se estrellaban a cuatrocientos metros.
Dieron la orden de avanzar.
Yo estaba envuelto en un bejucal.
Salimos a unos potreros
el monte nos tapaba hasta la rodilla
y los aviones pasaban cerca.
Yo grité enojado: esto es un atentado, nos traen de lo boscoso
a esto que está limpio. Y vos, Martín, gritaste: no tengan miedo
cuando el avión pase cerca siéntense y no se muevan.
Corriendo y sentándonos llegamos a la quebrada
allí te quitaste los zapatos y como veías el desespero de nosotros
con toda tranquilidad dijiste:
si nos cae una bomba hasta allí llegaremos
pero nadie se va a correr.
Estuvimos hasta las cuatro de la tarde. A las seis íbamos
llegando a la casa que ordenaste tomáramos.
Yo me asusté y tímidamente te pregunté
¿no le vamos a hacer nada a esta gente?
Y vos respondiste en tono afirmativo: NO.
Allí compraste un cerdo y dos gallinas.
La noche estuvo lluviosa
nos acostamos en los ranchos donde dormían las gallinas.
El compañero Malicia temblaba de fiebre
y no teníamos cobijas.
La noche siguiente íbamos de regreso
descartada la posibilidad de atacar el comando de Rivas.
En la carretera te tomó preso un guardia civil
y te deportó a Panamá
hasta que te volví a ver en el campamento
dirigiendo los ejercicios de las cinco a las seis de la mañana
y por la tarde dando charla política.
Recuerdo que por vos no me mandaron a otro campamento.

And I remember that because of you
they didn't send me to another camp.
After that I lost track of you
until I heard the news
that the Guardia of the tyrant had killed you in a firefight,
and heard you named "the priest Gaspar García Laviana."
Back when I knew you I didn't know you were a priest;
for me you were just a good leader,
devoted body and soul to the people's struggle.

YOUR INDIFFERENCE BUGS ME MORE

Your indifference bugs me more
than Gloria shouting "Son of the Great Whore!"
because of the wooden armadillo I failed to lay at her door.

FELIPE PEÑA was well known in Solentiname as a singer and songwriter; he
was also witty and outspoken. He and his father Tomás both contributed fre-
quently to the communal discussions of the Gospels (see *The Gospel in Solen-
tiname.*) During the assault on the National Guard garrison at San Carlos,
Felipe was captured because he stayed in position to cover the retreat of his
friends. He was tortured and held at La Bartolina prison in San Carlos for
almost a year until Eden Pastora's August 1978 raid on the National Palace in
Managua and the taking of congressional hostages forced the release of
political prisoners throughout Nicaragua. Felipe was flown to Panama, then
returned to Nicaragua via Costa Rica. He died in combat in the Nueva Guinea
district; his body was never found. Bosco Centeno has paid tribute to him in
"Felipe Peña" (see Appendix). The selection printed here shows the evolution
of his style from the simplicity of the early workshop exercises to the com-
plexity of the battle and prison poems.

Desde entonces no supe nada de vos
hasta que oí la noticia
que la guardia del tirano te habia matado en un combate
con tu nombre de sacerdote Gaspar García Laviana.
Cuando te conocí no sabía que eras cura
para mí eras un buen dirigente
entregado en cuerpo y alma a la lucha del pueblo.

TU INDIFERENCIA ME JODE MÁS

Tu indiferencia me jode más
que los hijueputazos de la Gloria
por el cusuco de madera que no le di.

ELVIS CHAVARRÍA

I WATCH THE WAVES BREAK

I watch the waves break.
A flock of herons passes.
Three ibises like women
seated on a rock.
A boat goes past, like a feather
between the waves.

THEY CARRIED THE WOUNDED CAMPESINO

They carried the wounded campesino
down to his farm.
Guardsmen had really worked him over.
Down from the thick mountains.
Dying, dying.
The wind ceaselessly moving the bushes.
There on the far horizon
the sun dropped out of sight.

THE FOAM

The foam flows following
the current of the lake.
White as milk fresh in the milking pail.
It flows, piles up, it looks like heaps of snow along the shoreline.
As it flow to Mancarrón, so it flows
to La Cigüeña, then on to La Carlota:
like great highways across the lake.

MIRO EL REVENTAR DE LAS OLAS

Miro el reventar de las olas.
Una bandada de garzas pasa
Tres cocas como damas
sentadas en una roca.
Un bote pasa como pluma
entre las olas.

AL CAMPESINO HERIDO LO LLEVARON

Al campesino herido lo llevaron
a su rancho.
Guardias lo jalaban.
Bajaron de las espesas montañas.
Moribundo, moribundo.
El viento sigue moviendo los breñales.
Allá en el lejano horizonte
el sol se ocultó.

LA ESPUMA

La espuma corre según la
corriente del lago.
Blanca como leche recién ordeñada.
Corre, arrima, ya en la costa
parece montones de nieve.
Mientras corre a Mancarrón, corre a la
Cigüeña, sigue a la Carlota:
parecen grandes caminos en el lago.

KATYDIDS, GÜISES, KESTRELS

Katydids, güises, kestrels
sing at nightfall.
Parrots fly by to their nests
up there on the hillside.
Night comes in.
Pocoyos, owls, frogs, crickets;
a kingfisher with his croaking song.
In his hut, Alberto says: "Dry spell coming."
Night passes softly.
Suddenly cocks crow.
Dawn breaks.
And there's the warbling of all the birds.
Juan says: "Compadre, you hear the punco sing last night?"
"Sure did, compadre."
"Then I reckon we better not plant."

WINTER

The widowbirds sing on all the farms
announcing summer.
From branch to branch among the trees
with their black bills and yellow breasts
they sing and sing all morning.

CHICHARRAS, GÜISES, GAVILANES

Chicharras, güises, gavilanes
cantan al anochecer.
Loras pasan volando a su dormitorio,
allá en una loma.
Entra la noche.
Pocoyos, lechuzas, ranas, grillos;
un martín-peña con su ronco cántico.
Alberto en su rancho dice: — va a haber sequía.
La noche transcurre quieta.
De repente gallos cantan.
Amanece.
Y se oye el trinar de todos los pájaros.
Juan dice: — Compadre ¿oyó anoche cantar el punco?
— Sí compadre. — Entonces, no hay que sembrar.

INVIERNO

Las "viudas" cantan en todos los potreros
anunciando verano.
En las ramas de los maderos
con su pico negro y su pecho amarillo
cantan y cantan toda la mañana.

SUMMER

You see the pink of the madero in flower,
the reddish-orange of the elequeme,
the iguana running;
the deep yellow of the poroporo,
leafy green of the sonzonate;
the fields already dry;
the tortoises already lumbering up to lay their eggs.
Smell of pinol de iguana on every farm.
Dried fish hung out in people's yards.
The sun strong, the mountain dry.
Agoutis at the foot of the coyol palm.
Hummingbirds flitting from flower to flower.
It's the time of year for hog plums, mangos, cashews,
and almíbar fruit cup, here in Solentiname.

LOVE IN THE COUNTRYSIDE

Güises who chatter to güisas.
The praying mantis who eats her lovers.
The billing and cooing of he-dove to she-dove.
Katydids chanting all day calling their katydads.
Fireflies that light themselves up in search of their loves.
Butterflies flying along on their wedding nights.
Crickets who sing long songs so their darlings will come.
Toads who call out to those they love best.
Great rings of gnats circling above the trees.
How full the whole countryside is with love.

VERANO

Se mira el rosado de la flor del madero,
el rojo naranja del elequeme;
el correr de la iguana;
amarillo intenso del poroporo,
verde frondoso del sonzonate.
Los llanos ya secos;
las tortugas ya están subiendo a desovar.
Olor a pinol de iguana en cada rancho.
Los pescados secos colgando en los patios.
El sol fuerte, el monte seco.
Las guatuzas bajo los palos de coyol.
Los gorriones brincando de flor en flor.
Es el tiempo de los jocotes, mangos, marañones,
y del almíbar en Solentiname.

AMOR EN EL CAMPO

Güises que picotean a sus güisas.
Mantis religiosa que se come a sus amados.
Con su ternura los palomos arrullan a sus palomas.
Chicharras que cantan todo el día llamando a sus chicharros.
Quiebra-platas que alumbran en busca de sus amores.
Mariposas que vuelan en sus noches de bodas.
Grillos que cantan largas tonadas para que vengan sus amadas.
Sapos que llaman a sus preferidas.
Chayules en grandes ruedas sobre los árboles.
De cuanto amor está lleno el campo.

SAN CARLOS

The water falls over the ramshackle rooftops.
An old woman cries: "Fried fish! Fried fish!"
Dogs, cats, pigs in the filthy street.
A pushcart with a bell, and an old man:
"Come and get 'em! Come and get 'em! Ice cream cones!"
Cantinas, barbershops, poolrooms,
gas stations, greasy spoons, whorehouses,
swallows, gnats, flies, the stench,
in the stalls everyone buying and selling, more stench, stalls, turds,
stench, Somoza on a poster shat on by swallows.
The clotheslines cluttered: sheets, shirts, pants, blouses,
the smashing sound of the women washing:
pon, pa, pon, pa, washing and washing.
Papayas, apples, mangos, cheese, stew,
watermelon, iced drinks, malteds.
More stalls, more gnats, swallows,
more turds, more posters.

SOLITUDE

It's a quarter of nine.
I can hear the rasping buzz of the crickets.
The sound of a motor.
You're not here.
I think of a girl, I remember her face
and I say to myself: "How lovely."
A girl who travels by motor launch mounting and sliding down
        wave after wave.
I remember I need to scare up some "rondon"
a dish made of mountain pork, yucca, plantains, tiquisque,
and as always I'm alone.

SAN CARLOS

El agua cae sobre los techos corroídos.
Una vieja dice: pescado frito, pescado frito.
Perros, gatos, chanchos, en la calle bien sucia.
Un carretón con una campanilla, y un viejo:
a ver, a ver, aquí están los conos.
Cantinas, barberías, billares,
gasolineras, comiderias, putales.
Golondrinas, chayules, moscas, tufo,
mercadeo, más tufo, mercadeo, cagadas,
tufo, Somoza en un afiche cagado de golondrinas.
Cordeles repletos: sábanas, camisas, pantalones, blusas,
el golpe de las mujeres: pon, pa, pon, pa,
lavando, y siguen lavando.
Los mamones, las manzanas, los mangos, el queso, el vajo,
la sandía, el fresco helado, la horchata.
Más mercadeo, más chayules, golondrinas,
más cagadas, más afiches.

SOLEDAD

Falta un cuarto para las nueve.
Escucho el chillar de los grillos.
El sonar del motor.
Vos no estás.
Pienso en una muchacha, recuerdo su cara
y me digo: qué linda.
Una muchacha navegando en una lancha, bajando o subiendo cada ola.
Recuerdo que tengo que pescar un "rondón,"
comida que lleva carne de chancho de monte, yuca, plátano, tiquisque,
y siempre estoy solo.

LATE AFTERNOON IN SOLENTINAME

A dark shadow over an island.
In the sky a clarity of reds,
oranges, lilacs, violets.
A world of color alone.
And I alone in the world.

RIO PAPATURRO

Here come the herons, their eyes fixed on the water.
Howler monkeys croon
lazily snuggled together in a deep all-day sleep.
On a branch, a fisherbird all gay colors,
eyes fixed on passing sardines.
Herons, howlers, songbirds
along the streams that feed the Rio Papaturro
announce the new day.

AT NIGHT

At night
in Solentiname
you can hear the singing of the pocoyos
the gru-gru-grunting of the toads,
while in a house
right at the edge of the lake
silence reigns.

ATARDECER EN SOLENTINAME

Una sombra oscura en una isla.
En el cielo una claridad de rojos
naranjas, lilas, violetas.
Un solo mundo de colores.
Y yo solo en el mundo.

RÍO PAPATURRO

Se ven garzas, con su mirada fija en el agua.
Congos cantan; perezosos, acurrucados
con un sueño profundo de todo el día.
En una rama un pájaro pescador con colores alegres
mirada fija en sardinas que pasa.
Garzas, congos, pájaros,
en las riveras del río Papaturro
anuncian el nuevo día.

EN LAS NOCHES

En las noches
en Solentiname
se escuchan los cantidos de los pocoyos
el ronroneo de los sapos
mientras en una casa
que está en la orilla del lago
reina el silencio.

YOU'RE FAR FROM SOLENTINAME

You passed through like the wind.
Quickly oh so quickly
like the armored cars
of the tyrant.

FISHING

The lake calm.
We two fishing.
The boat's ripples breaking
the peace of the lake.
We came to the spot where we were going to fish.
We were very quiet.
Suddenly you shouted,
up through the air a fish flopped into the boat.
In the distance we could make out Ometepe Island
with its two peaks.
Another fish. Another shout.
The lake remained like a mirror.

NIGHT

A black night in the month of July.
You hear the sad song of the pocoyo.
The glittering of thousands of fireflies
makes it look like a great city.
But no: it's a night in Solentiname.

ELVIS CHAVARRÍA, son of Natalia Sequeira, was born on the island that now bears his name. He was admired as a calm, patient person and a great athlete; children especially loved him. He was captured during the raid on San Carlos, taken up the Rio Frío, and shot in the head. See Bosco Centeno's "To Elvis Chavarría" (Appendix).

ESTÁS LEJOS DE SOLENTINAME

Pasaste como el viento.
Rápido tan rápido
como los carros blindados
del tirano.

LA PESCA

El lago calmo.
Nosotros dos de pesca.
El bote rompe la tranquilidad del lago
con sus pequeñas olas.
Llegamos al sitio donde íbamos a pescar.
Estábamos callados.
De repente gritaste,
en el aire un pescado cayó al bote.
Lejos se veía la Isla Ometepe
con sus dos cerros.
Otro pescado. Otro grito.
El lago seguía como un espejo.

NOCHE

Una noche negra del mes de julio.
Se oye el canto triste de un pocoyo.
El relumbrar de miles de quiebra-platas
parece una gran ciudad.
Pero no, es una noche en Solantiname.

DÓNALD GUEVARA

CATTLE

The cattle run leap kick up their heels
as the sun heats up the fields.
When night arrives
they gather into a single unit,
forming a solid mass.
The cow, recently calved, raises her ears
and sniffs the calf, caressing it with her tongue.
Through the deep hours of the night
the steer chews some remnant of fodder
in its extended muzzle while
it rests, worn out from a day spent wandering.
Dawn, the calf bellows
in search of its mother
whose udder at this hour is like an enormous keg
full of water
and the four teats give it the shape of some
notable native bowl.
The calf moves its grubby little snout
desperately mouthing the teats
bloated with milk.
When the enormous udder is emptied
by the vigorous sucking and gulping
the calf gives it with his flat face
the rigid teats go soft and shrink
like those little plastic bags of
orangeade a kid sucks dry.

IN THE DARK NIGHT

In the dark night
a star or two up there
we could hear the phonograph in the distance
while I gave you a hand getting into your boat
that was still empty
and ever so slowly like a clump of grass floating downstream
you were lost in the darkness
without saying when we would ever meet again.

60

LOS VACUNOS

El ganado corre brinca patea
mientras el sol calienta los campos.
Al llegar la noche
se echan en un solo conjunto
formando un manchón injerto.
Las hembras paridas levantan sus orejas
y olfatean su ternero acariciándolo con la lengua.
Durante las horas profundas de la noche
el adulto rumea los residuos de alimentos
que le quedan en su alargada trompa mientras
descansa de su agotador andar.
Al llegar la madrugada los terneros berrean
en busca de su madre
que a la misma hora tiene la ubre como una enorme pipa
llena de agua,
y los cuatro pezones que la dan su forma como
una importante vasija indígena.
El ternero coloca su fea trompa
acariciando desesperadamente los pezones
henchidos de leche.
Cuando la enorme pipa ya está vacía
a costa de los fuertes chupetazos y golpes
que el ternero le da con su redonda frente,
los tiesos pezones disminuyen
y van quedando como unas pequeñas chuspas
de naranja exprimidas (desjugadas).

EN LA NOCHE OSCURA

En la noche oscura
una que otra estrella;
el tocadisco ya se oía algo lejos,
mientras te daba la mano para bajar al bote
que aún estaba vacío
y despacio como un gamalote te fuiste perdiendo
sin decir cuándo nos volveríamos a ver.

BITTERNESS

Before lying down to dream
I look out my window
the night black
as your desires.

BITTER HOUR

With the shadow of the moon
across my feet
and my throat dry
I remember the night
you kissed me.

THE OLD DESERTED TAVERN

On the far side of the long bay
all I can see is the doorway of the old cantina
rising above the dark green of the caliguatales
and the little yard where as a kid I used to spin my top
has all gone to brambles near the grove of coconut palms
that I myself watched grow.
Chon, Gil and Lolo no longer stroll by
in search of that famous rotgut rum
and that white lightning cut with water and lime
that Santos sold them.
No more hearing Oscar holding forth
nor the strumbrrumm! of the old guitar
that kept the first roosters company at dawn.
Now it's all silence.
Only Santos is left with his mop of white hair
and his smiling hermit's face;
he serves his friends and doesn't sell a drop.

AMARGURA

Antes de soñar
por mi ventana miro
la noche negra
como tus placeres.

AMARGA HORA

Con la sombra de la luna
en mis pies
y la garganta seca
recuerdo la noche
que me besaste.

LA ANTIGUE CANTINA

Al otro lado de la larga ensenada
sólo miro el umbral de la ranchita
sobre el verde-oscuro de los caliguatales,
y la placita donde de niño jugaba trompo
está enzarzada junto con los cocos que miré crecer.
Ya no desfilan Chon, Gil y Lolo
en busca de la famosa cususa
y del alcohol con agua y limón
que Santos les vendía.
Tampoco se oyen las discusiones de Oscar
ni el cherrenguechén de la vieja guitarra
que acompañaba a los primeros gallos.
Ahora es un silencio.
Sólo está Santos con su cabellera blanca
y su rostro risueño de ermitaño;
hace servicios a sus amigos sin vender un solo trago.

LIFE IN SOLENTINAME

Solentiname
little archipelago in the lake
where the poet gives
a special flavor to his poems.
Because of the immense silence
all you can hear is the "güir! güir!" of the cormorants
the song of the güises
the clarion call of the zanates
the noisy ruckus of the tijules
when the chocoyo reaches their fledglings
the crashing of waves against the stone coasts
that are the start and finish of every island
where tortoises lumber by to enjoy the hot rays of the sun.
All I see and hear is a rowboat
that from a distance some outsider might mistake
for a heap of drifting water hyacinth
but which is really my darling Mimí
gone fishing.

NIGHT

I think our nature is very solid in Solentiname,
with its incomparable courage like love
and I mean a truly human love.
I wait for dawn in the silent night
and all I hear are the pocollos singing "Joíojoío!"
Even they know who's going to get the shaft.

DÓNALD GUEVARA, one of the nine children of doña Olivia Silva and don Julio Guevara, was a hardworking young man: fishing, farming, building, boating, he did it all. His sister Mariita remembers him as a boy who was "always dreaming about the future." Along with Elvis Chavarría, Dónald was captured during the assault on San Carlos, taken up the Río Frío, and shot. A new vocational school has been named for him in Solentiname. See the tribute from his brother-in-law Bosco Centeno, "Dónald" (Appendix).

VIDA EN SOLENTINAME

Solentiname
pequeño archipiélago del lago
lugar donde el poeta
da sabor a sus poesías.
A causa de su silencio inmenso
sólo se escucha el güir de los patos chanchos,
el canto de los güises
y el clarín de los zanates
y el escándalo de los tijules
cuando la chocalla llega a sus pichones
el romper de las olas contra las empedradas costas
que dan origen y final a cada isla
donde las tortugas pasan y disfrutan de los calientes rayos del sol.
Sólo miro y escucho un bote de remos
que a lo lejos alguien, extraño, pudiera creer que es
alguna lechuga de río que va a la deriva
y es mi querida Mimí
que va de pesca.

NOCHE

Pienso qué concreta es la naturaleza en Solentiname.
Con su valor incomparable como un amor
y un amor de veras humano.
Yo espero amanecer en la silenciosa noche
y sólo escucho a los pocollos que cantan joíojoío.
Hasta ellos saben quién será el jodido.

BOSCO CENTENO

FEBRUARY SQUALLS

Violent February squalls
herons and ducks search in vain for a sheltered pool
where they can fish
the little boats appear and disappear
and the swallows skimming over the waves without getting wet
the flight of the egrets lifted by the wind
and the sky like a distant stubblefield in flames.

MEMORIES OF YOU

Memories of you are now like flashes of lightning:
at first I thought they'd be like a sun,
but soon they'll grow dark as night.

IF YOU WANTED ME

If you wanted me as much as you said you did
you'll go on loving me in silence
even though you may think I've already forgotten you.

THE OROPÉNDOLA

The oropéndola on
the branch of the genízaro
pecks hungrily
at the red flesh
of a pitaya;
my presence
interrupts her meal
and, startled,
she flies off screeching.

CHUBASCOS DE FEBRERO

Chubascos de Febrero violentos
las garzas y los patos buscan en vano un remanso donde pescar
los botecitos aparecen y desaparecen
y las golondrinas volando sobre las olas sin mojarse
el vuelo de las garzas llevadas por el viento
y el cielo como un rastrojo lejano en llamas.

TUS RECUERDOS

Tus recuerdos ahora son como relámpagos;
antes creí que serían como un sol,
pero pronto serán como la noche.

SI ME QUISISTE

Si me quisiste como me decías
aun me amarás en silencio
aunque pienses que ya te olvidé.

LA OROPÉNDOLA

La oropéndola en
la rama del genízaro
picotea hambrienta
la roja carne
de una pitaya;
mi presencia
interrumpe su comida
y asustada
se aleja
        chillando.

THE ANAHINGAS

The anahingas with
long dark bills
quack and display
and snatch sardines from the water.
The males quarrel and scrap.
The females, more slender and delicate,
and with longer webfeet
stay in the branches
with wings spread to the sun,
and fall asleep.
And the nearly bald black chicks
open their bills waiting for food
on the big island
all day long.

LIKE THE QUICK LEAP OF THE TARPON

Like the quick leap of the tarpon on May afternoons
and the shooting stars on summer nights:
just so was our love.

REMEMBER

Remember that life is not even
a thousandth of a second in the great sweep of time:
but one kiss from you is enough to make it all stand still.

THE SENZONTLE

The senzontle plays in a corozo palm
then suddenly flies toward the distant song of his mate;
the palm is left swaying.

LOS PATOS

Los patos-agujas con el
pico largo y negro
graznan y papalean,
cogen las sardinas del agua.
Y los machos pelean.
Los patos hembras más estilizados y fines
y con el bolillo más largo,
que están en las ramas
con las alas tendidas al sol,
se duermen.
Y los críos negros pelones
abren el pico esperando su comida
en el islote
todo el día.

COMO EL SALTO RÁPIDO DEL SÁBALO

Como el salto rápido del sábalo en las tardes de mayo
y las estrellas fugaces en noches de verano:
así fue nuestro amor.

RECORDÁ

Recordá que la vida no es siquiera
una milésima de segundo en el tiempo.
Pero un beso tuyo basta para detenerlo.

EL SENZONTLE

El senzontle juega en una palma de corozo
y rápido vuela hacia el canto lejano de la hembra
la palma queda meciéndose.

TYRANT, FEAR THE POETS

Tyrant, fear the poets
because neither with your Sherman tanks
nor with your fighter planes
nor with your combat battalions
nor with your security forces
nor with your Nicolasa
nor with your 40 thousand marines
nor with your super-trained rangers
nor even with your God
will you avoid being shot as this story unfolds.

AN EGRET

An egret goes slowly by
lazily moving her wings
seeing her image
on the calm surface of the lake.

THE GARROBO

The big green garrobo
who lived at the top
of the breadnut tree
and who always hid himself
among the leaves,
well I finally managed to catch him
and tomorrow
we're gonna eat him
in a rich cornmeal-thickened lizardmeat stew.

TENLE MIEDO A LOS POETAS TIRANO

Tenle miedo a los poetas tirano
porque ni con tus tanques sherman
ni con tus aviones a reacción
ni con tu batallón de combate
ni con tu seguridad
ni con tu nicolasa
ni con cuarenta mil marines
ni con tus super-entrenados ránger
ni siquiera tu Dios
evitará que te fusilen en la historia.

UNA GARZA

Una garza va despacio
moviendo perezosamente sus alas
viéndose
retratada sobre la calmura del lago.

EL GARROBO

El gran garrobo lapo
que vivía en la cumbrita
del palo de ojoche
y que se confundía siempre
entre sus hojas,
al fin lo pude coger
y mañana
lo comeremos
en rico pinol.

WE'LL BE ABLE

We'll be able, hand in hand
to stroll fearless along the curve of the universe
at that time
when the energy of our love is released.

LITTLE HEARTBREAKER

Little heartbreaker
who at 13 swore me your love,
now that you're 18, you call me "Señor"
even though you still remember the promise
we couldn't keep.

THE EGRETS

The egrets fly on toward the island of grass
the ducks to their havens;
we two in each other's arms
to the song of the pocoyo
await the moon.

YOU CHAT, YOU SWEEP, YOU TIDY UP

You chat, you sweep, you tidy up, completely unselfconscious,
without realizing perhaps that the sweet jugs
of your breasts keep trying to hide themselves from my gaze.

PODREMOS

Podremos, tomados de la mano
dar un paseo por la curvatura del universo
sin miedo al tiempo
cuando la energía de nuestro amor se libere.

NIÑA CRUEL

Niña cruel
que a los trece me juraste amor
hoy tenés dieciocho, me decís señor
aunque recordás la promesa
que no pudimos cumplir.

LAS GARZAS

Las garzas pasan al Zacatón
los patos a sus dormideros;
nosotros abrazados
con el canto del pocoyo
esperamos la luna.

PLATICÁS, BARRÉS, ARREGLÁS

Platicás, barrés, arreglás, despreocupada
sin darte cuenta, tal vez, que las tinajitas
de tus pechos intentan esconderse de mi mirada.

EVERYTHING WILL BE DIFFERENT

Everything will be different when the revolution triumphs.
Love for the people will be our love.
But we two will love each other just the same.

WHEN THE ENERGY OF OUR LOVE IS RELEASED

When the energy of our love is released
and fearless of time we voyage through infinity
and are perhaps the sperm and ovary of a new planet
we will still remember our first kiss.

YOU WERE BORN TO BE A POET'S SWEETHEART

You were born to be a poet's sweetheart
and I love to watch you so much
that your breasts seem to me like the tender fruit of the nispero.
I could write your name,
I could write so many things
but girl,
you're my best friend's sweetheart
and these verses will remain my secret.

LINES WRITTEN ON A BASEBALL

Yesterday, quick as one of Vinnie's hardballs,
you smiled and said that while you knew nothing about playing ball
you thought I had played well.
Girl,
getting you to smile like that
has been my best play yet.

TODO SERÁ DISTINTO

Todo será distinto cuando triunfe la revolución.
El amor al pueblo será nuestro amor.
Pero nosotros dos nos amaremos lo mismo.

CUANDO LA ENERGÍA DE NUESTRO AMOR SE LIBERE

Cuando la energía de nuestro amor se libere
y recorramos el infinito sin miedo al tiempo
y tal vez seamos espermatozoide y óvulo de un nuevo planeta
aun recordaremos nuestro primer beso.

QUE NACISTE PARA SER NOVIA

Que naciste para ser la novia de un poeta
y me gusta tanto mirarte
que tus pechos parecen nisperos tiernos.
Podría escribir tu nombre
podría escribir tantas cosas más
pero muchacha
sos la novia de mi amigo
y estos verso serán mi secreto.

ESCRITO EN UNA PELOTA DE BÉISBOL

Ayer rápidamente como un lanzamiento de Vincent
sonriendo decías que aunque no sabías de pelota
yo había jugado muy bien.
Muchacha
esa tu sonrisa
ha sido mi mejor jugada.

IN THE BUS

Your palmfrond-colored eyes
grab me and leave me helpless
like a bird face to face with a boa.
I can't seem to tear myself away
although you laugh, enjoying the game
and I begin to compose these verses
which you will likely never know about
just as I will likely never know your name.

EXILE

That güis up there perched
on a TV antenna
is singing, like me,
a sad song.
All the same, tomorrow we two will sing
in some great-branching tree.

THIS MOON HALF-HIDDEN

This moon half-hidden
among neon signs
between huge buildings of cement and steel
makes it hard for me to imagine
this same moon is rising between island and lake
in front of my house in Solentiname.
Here there's only cars, motorcycles, racket
and there's no way I can pretend it's
the sound of the lake
or the song of the pocoyo
or the screech owl.

EN EL BUS

Tus ojos color de palmeras
me atraen indefenso como
pájaro frente a una boa.
Imposible apartarme
aunque te riás haciéndote gracia el juego
y comience a hacerte estos versos
que nunca conozcás,
y yo jamás sepa tu nombre.

EXILIO

Ese güis sentado
en una antena de televisión
está cantando igual que yo
una canción triste.
Aunque mañana cantaremos
en un árbol de grandes ramas.

ESTA LUNA QUE SE CONFUNDE

Esta luna que se confunde
con anuncios de neón
entre grandes edificios de hierro y cemento
me cuesta creer que sale entre islas y lago
frente a mi casa en Solentiname.
Aquí hay carros, motos, ruidos
y no los siento como al rumor del lago
el canto del pocoyo y la lechuza.

I REMEMBER, GIRL

I remember, girl, the blue color of your hammock
with your bare smooth body
like the blossom of the pitahaya that bursts open at dawn
or like the little dove of San Nicolás
trembling with fear between my hands;
the unwelcome lantern swarming with gnats,
the noise of the launch's motor that kept us from talking;
and I even remember the date of your birthday.
But so much time has passed
that perhaps you may be reading these lines
and not know they were for you.

YOU

You look great wearing your fashionable clothes
along the Avenida Central
but even better in camp
in your uniform, with your rifle.

JUST AS A TAPIR

Just as a tapir
wrenches itself free
from the jaguar's grip
by leaving behind some of its claws
so I ripped the memory of you
trembling like a startled doe
out of my mind
though it was you
who carried away
some part of me.

YO RECUERDO MUCHACHA

Yo recuerdo muchacha el color azul de tu hamaca
con tu cuerpo desnudo y suave
como una flor de pitahaya que revienta al amanecer
y como una palomita San Nicolás
asustada entre mis manos.
La bujía inoportuna llena de chayules
el ruido del motor del lanchón que nos impedía hablar
y recuerdo hasta la fecha de tu cumpleaños.
Pero ha pasado tanto tiempo
que tal vez leás estos versos
y no sepás que fueron para vos.

VOS

Bonita vos con tu vestido a la moda
por la Avenida Central
pero más bonita sos en el campamento
con el uniforme y tu fusil.

COMO UN DANTO

Como un danto se desprende del tigre
dejándole parte de sus uñas
así arranqué tu recuerdo de
venadita asustada
aunque te llevaste parte de mí.

HIDING OURSELVES IN THE NIGHT

Hiding ourselves in the night up among the mountains
like jaguars ready to pounce
hearing the quickening thump of our hearts
mosquitos go by making airplane noises
we don't feel them when they bite
rifle loaded and ready, safety off
pulse strong and steady
and the outlines of the helmets go by and a rifle
and another and yet another . . .
and a shot, followed by a volley, and the mountain sounds go silent
and "Viva Sandino!" and "Viva Monimbó!"
"Patria Libre o Morir!"
the dust drying your throat
time stretching out and the silence broken by
cries that beg for mercy . . .
coming out of the bushes, still alert and ready,
we gather up guns and documents
patch up the wounded guardsmen
and silently slip away into the mountains.

SWEATY AND MUDDY

Sweaty and muddy
three days of march, four of ambush
pale, body covered with bites
backpack weighing you down like a cross
slowly passing the checkpoints of the camp
the faces of the compañeros ask us:
"Everybody OK?"
"Compañero, not a single shot in seven days
nothing to tell."
Tomorrow other compañeros will go out on ambush.

EN LA NOCHE CONFUNDIDOS

En la noche confundidos entre el monte
igual que tigres al acecho
oyéndonos el latido acelerado del corazón
zancudos pasando con ruidos de aviones
no se sienten sus piquetes
el fusil bala en boca, sin seguro
con pulso firme decidido
y pasan sombras de casco y fusil una y otra y otra otra . . .
y el disparo, seguido de muchos más, callan los sonidos de la montaña
y vivas a Sandino a Monimbó
de Patria Libre o Morir
la pólvora que reseca la garganta,
alargándose el tiempo y el silencio rotos por
gritos pidiendo clemencia
saliendo de los matorrales siempre al acecho
recogiendo fusiles, documentos
curamos a los guardias heridos
y silenciosos desaparecemos en la montaña.

SUDOROSOS Y ENLODADOS

Sudorosos y enlodados
tres días de marcha y cuatro emboscando
pálidos, con el cuerpo lleno de piquetes
la mochila pesando como una cruz
pasando las postas del campamento despacio,
compañeros con la mirada nos preguntan:
¿Todos completos? Compañero ni un tiro en siete días
nada de contar.
Otros compañeros saldrán mañana a emboscar.

BROTHER GUARDSMAN, FORGIVE ME

Brother guardsman, forgive me for having to take
careful aim so I can shoot you
but hospitals depend on our shots,
and the schools we never had
where your kids will play with ours.
Know this: all these will justify our shots
but what you've done will be
your generation's shame.

TO MY WIFE, ESPERANZA

The moonlight that filters between these upland branches
and glints off the lean-to brings you to my mind.
I think that, there in San Juan among the Christmas lights,
you'll hardly see this moon, beautiful as the revolution,

or I think that perhaps our glances might be fused
somewhere in heaven,

or I think that perhaps you might be weeping to remember me
not knowing if I'm alive,
and our daughters might be
playing grown-up, with your shoes, in the living room.
You understand, my love, that our suffering
at this historic moment is a kind of satisfaction.

SOLENTINAME

Solentiname was Julio Guevara with his fishing pole and his laugh,
    pulling fish from the lake.
It was the girls lined up in their rowboats, like sprays of blossoms,
    going to Mass.
And the egrets along the shore — as Alejandro says: From a distance
    you could mistake them for Virgins.
And fiestas, and we drinking a shot or two under the mango tree
    across from the church, listening to Chono's phonograph.

82

HERMANO GUARDIA, PERDONÁ

Hermano guardia perdoná que tenga que afinar
bien la puntería al dispararte,
pero de nuestros disparos dependen los hospitales
y las escuelas que no tuvimos,
donde jugarán tus hijos con los nuestros.
Sabé que ellos justificarán nuestros disparos
pero los hechos por vos serán
vergüenza de tu generación.

A ESPERANZA MI MUJER

La luna que se filtra entre las ramas de la montaña
y se refleja en la champa, me trae tu recuerdo.
Pienso que en San José entre luces de Navidad
apenas verás esta luna hermosa como la revolución,
o que tal vez nuestras miradas estén juntas
en algún lugar del cielo
o tal vez estés llorando al recordarme sin saber
si estoy vivo,
y nuestras hijas estarán jugando
a las señoras, con tus zapatos en la sala.
Vos comprendés, amor, que nuestra pena
en este momento histórico es una satisfacción.

SOLENTINAME

Solentiname fue Julio Guevara con su vara de madroño y su risa,
sacando peces del lago.
Fue las muchachas arregladitas en sus botes de remos, como
            ramos de flores
yendo a misa.
Y las garzas en la costa que como dice Alejandro: De lejos se pueden
confundir con una virgen.
Y las fiestas con los tragos bajo los palos de mango frente a la
iglesia con el tocadisco de Chono.

It was everybody in town discussing the Gospels on Sunday.
And expeditions to find tortoises and lizards to bring back for our
    communal lunches.
And the music of Elvis, William and Adancito on Sundays.
And the shouts of children aboard boats on the way to school
    scaring away the ducks, who took flight shitting.
Solentiname was our oath of "Patria Libre o Morir!"
And Ernesto prophesying a New Age and a New Earth.
And the Company monopolizing all the land.
And the canvases of our campesino painters, crammed with life.
Solentiname is Julio Guevara in exile with his smile
    glimpsing the future
It's Elvis and Dónald, captured, their heads bloodied, trussed up
    like burlap bags in the launch and taken toward Managua
    (that's the last we ever saw of them).
It's Felipe captured in San Carlos, kept like an oriole in a cage,
    unable to write.
It's Sunday like any other day.
It's José and Oscar tortured by the ranger Franklin Montenegro.
It's the memory of our islands.
(It's the egret along the shore that, from a distance, you could
    mistake for a Virgin.)
It's our homes against which the Somocistas vented that rage of the
    impotent mighty.
It's the kids staying home because there are no schools.
It's the pain you have to go through to give life.
Solentiname will be Julio Guevara with his laugh and his
    grandchildren, hauling in fish from the lake.
And the distant egrets resembling Virgins.
And the cries of children on their way to the school of the revolution
    scaring off defecating ducks.
And the Company lands transformed into livestock cooperatives.
And "Yes, Compañero Machetero," and
    "Yes, Compañero Field Hand,"
    "Yes, Compañero."
Every day it will be Sunday and a Mass.
It will be
        it will be
                it will be
                        it will be
to each according to his needs.

Fue el pueblo discutiendo el evangelio los domingos.
Y las idas a coger tortugas y garrobos para nuestros
   almuerzos comunales.
Y la música de Elvis, William y Adancito los domingos.
Y la bulla de los niños en los botes en camino de la escuela ahuyentando
patos que se levantaban cagando.
Solentiname fue nuestro juramento de Patria Libre o Morir.
Y Ernesto profetizando tiempos y tierras nuevas.
Y la Compañía monopolizando las tierras.
Y los cuadros llenos de vida de los pintores campesinos.
Solentiname es Julio Guevara en el exilio con su sonrisa
entreviendo el futuro.
Es Elvis y Dónald, presos con la capucha ensangrentada arpillados como
sacos en una lancha y llevados a Managua (no hemos vuelto a
   saber de ellos).
Es Felipe preso en San Carlos, como una chorcha en jaula
   sin poder escribir.
Es el domingo como un día más.
Es José y Oscar torturados por el ránger Franklin Montenegro.
Es el recuerdo de nuestras islas.
(Es la garza en la costa que de lejos se puede confundir con una virgen.)
Es nuestras casas donde saciaron su rabia de prepotentes impotentes.
Es los niños en las casas porque no hay escuelas.
Es el dolor que hay que tener para dar vida.
Solentiname será Julio Guevara con su risa y los nietos sacando peces
del lago.
Y las garzas de lejos semejando vírgenes.
Y los gritos de los niños espantando patos cagones
en camino para la escuela de la revolución.
Y las tierras de la Compañía convertidas en cooperativas ganaderas.
Y el sí compañero machetero, y sí compañero campisto, sí compañero.
Cada día será un domingo y una misa.
Será
     Será
          Será
               será a cada uno según sus necesidades.

FOR CHICHA (TONY) FALLEN IN NUEVA GUINEA

You used to say that for you death was
like a beautiful poem
and when you fell your blood soaked the kernels of corn
you kept in the pockets of your uniform
and from your body the seeds sprouted up
and grew into huge and mighty stalks.

RIVER GIRL

River girl
with your blue jeans and your sporty purse
sitting on a beer cooler
travelling on the launch
(that now belongs to the people)
your eyes fixed on the foamy wake
that the propeller leaves behind
holding down your beautiful hair
that plays about your face without makeup
your glance in my direction
mischievous and furtive
foreshadowing the moon that
this summer night I intend to show you.

A CHICHA (TONY) CAÍDO EN NUEVA GUINEA

Decías que para vos la muerte era
como un bello poema
y cuando caíste tu sangre regó las mazorcas de maíz
que llevabas en los bolsillos del uniforme
y sobre tu cuerpo puyoniaron los granos
y crecieron grandes y fuertes espigas.

MUCHACHA DEL RÍO

Muchacha del río
con tu bluyín y bolso deportivo
sentada en una hielera de cerveza
viajando en el lanchón
(que ahora es del pueblo)
la mirada fija en la estela de espuma
que deja el motor de la lancha
sosteniéndote el pelo
que juega hermoso en tu cara sin maquillar
tu mirada hacia mí
pícara y clandestina
presagiando la luna que
esta noche de verano voy a mostrarte.

I'M NOT GOING TO TELL YOU

I'm not going to tell you that the stars
we each see at the same moment
unite us somewhere in the Infinite,
or that we are somehow joined when we each hear love songs
we listened to when we were just kids in love.
Esperanza, our union is in those Luis Alfonso Velásquezes
who run safe and healthy throughout Nicaragua
and the compañera who sells pork and the compañero
who sells bread and the compañero who keeps guard on the bench
and we are united with them as in some electrical circuit
through which love flows.

BOSCO CENTENO was a frequent contributor to the discussions of the Gospel
in the early '70s in Solentiname. After the San Carlos raid he returned to com-
bat and fought until the triumph in 1979. He is currently military commander
of the San Juan River region; troops under his command shot down the plane
carrying Eugene Hasenfus. Of the original Solentiname poets, only Bosco and
his brother-in-law Iván Guevara are still writing and publishing poetry. His
Puyonearon los granos won the first Leonel Rugama Prize in 1981. See four
poems from this book in the Appendix. He is married to Esperanza Guevara
and lives in San Carlos.

NO VOY A DECIRTE

No voy a decirte que las estrellas
que miramos en un mismo instante
nos unen en algún lugar del infinito
o que nos encontramos al oir las canciones de amor
que escuchábamos cuando éramos novios.
Esperanza
nuestra unión es en los Luis Alfonso Velásquez
que corren sanos por todo Nicaragua
y la compañera vende-chancho y el compañero
que vende el pan y el compañero que hace posta
en los bancos
y estamos unidos a ellos como en un circuito eléctrico
donde fluye el amor.

GLORIA GUEVARA

AT THE TOP OF THE TOWN

The afternoon is grey and it's turning cold
and my soul's the same color as the afternoon.
I'm standing at the sill of an open window
at the top of the town.
From here I can see rooftops and banners
and farther off, mountains
like a wash of permanent green.
The sound equipment is going full blast
and I hear a song that moves me deeply,
bringing me back to my marvelous archipelago,
that song called "The Coplas of Compadre Juan Miguel"
that we used to sing with Elvis
sitting in the beached boat
on moonlit nights.

YOUNG MAN OF 20

I liked you better when I saw you
with your thick beard
long and black,
your blue cap,
your red shirt,
and your faded jeans.

DESDE EL ALTO DE LA COMUNIDAD

La tarde está de color gris y está haciendo mucho frío,
y mi alma del mismo color de esta tarde.
Estoy parada a orilla de una ventana
en el alto de la comunidad.
Desde aquí veo techos de casas y banderas
y allá más lejos montañas
como veladuras de verde permanente.
El equipo de sonido de aquí está prendido
y oigo una canción que me recuerda
con mucha profundidad
mi maravilloso archipiélago
aquella canción llamada Las Coplas del Compadre Juan Miguel
que cantábamos con Elvis en el bote
en media playa
en las noches de luna.

AL JOVEN DE VEINTE AÑOS

Me gustaste más cuando te miré
con tu tupida barba
larga y negra,
tu boina azul,
tu camisa roja,
y tu blue-jean descolorido.

MISERY

I came to a place
where they throw out
the whole town's garbage.

And I saw some kids
with some old sacks
they were filling with rusty cans
worn-out shoes
pieces of old cardboard box.

And some flies got into the sacks
and then they got out again
and settled down on the heads of the children.

WASHING CORN ON THE BEACH

I go down to the dark green guava tree
that grows at the edge of the beach
to wash corn for tortillas.

I strip down to get comfortable,
I'm only wearing my red panties.

I scrub the corn until it's white.
When I'm done, I wash my pink smock, I bathe
and then I go home.

EL PUEBLO EN MISERIA

Llegué a un lugar
donde botan todas
las basuras del pueblo.

Y miré a unos niños
con unos sacos viejos
que los llenaron de tarros oxidados,
zapatos rotos,
pedazos de cajas de cartón viejas.

Y unas moscas se les metían entre los sacos
y se volvían a salir
y se les sentaban en las cabezas.

LAVAR EL MAÍZ EN LA PLAYA

Me voy para el palo de guabo, verde oscuro,
que está a la orilla de la playa,
a lavar el maíz para las tortillas.

Me quito la ropa para sentirme más cómoda
y sólo he quedado con mi calzón rojo.

Restriego el maíz hasta dejarlo blanco.
Termino, lavo mi cotona rosada, me baño,
y me regreso.

FIRST KISS

I remember well the first time
you kissed me on the mouth
it was at the far end of the wharf
during that fiesta
under the mango trees
the night of March 19th.

THE GUERRILLERO

You who left the warmth of home
to seek the truest of all loves:

If they kill you
your death will not be in vain
because you will live
in the memory of the people.

THE SON

I want a son and I want to feel what it means to be a mother:
bathe him every day, dress him,
make him smell sweet, give him his cold drink
and his meals when the time comes round.
Study him carefully, decide which of us he resembles most,
me or my beloved.
Dream that when he grows up
he'll be a fighter for the freedom of the people.

ALREADY WITHERED

They're already withered
the red roses
you gave me
on my birthday.

94

EL PRIMER BESO

Recuerdo muy bien la primera vez
que me besaste en la boca
en la punta del muelle
cuando aquella fiesta
debajo de los palos de mango
la noche del 19 de marzo.

EL GUERRILLERO

Vos que dejaste el calor de tu hogar
para buscar el amor verdadero.

Si te matan tu muerte no será
en vano
porque vivirás en el recuerdo
del pueblo.

EL HIJO

Deseo un hijo, y el sentirme ser madre.
Bañarlo todos los días, vestirlo,
perfumarlo, darle su refresco,
y su comida a sus horas.
Contemplarlo, y distinguir a quién se parece
¿a mí o a mi amado?
Soñar que cuando esté grande
sea un combatiente por la liberación del pueblo.

YA SE MARCHITARON

Ya se marchitaron
las rosas rojas
que me regalaste
el día de mi cumpleaños.

ALCOHOLISM

I'm between the rocks
and the foulsmelling garbage from my village.
My clothes are filthy and torn,
my shoes are just about shot.
My color's bad and I stink,
everyone looks at me with scorn.
When I'm really drunk
I sing and shout.
My sisters, the flies, keep me company all day,
and mosquitos suck my blood all night.

LAST NIGHT I DREAMT

Last night I dreamt we had to transport
a large shipment of arms to Delicias on the San Juan de la Cruz
and bury them there;
but we had to take them away the next morning
because the enemy was coming in the afternoon.
The boat had two big holes in it
and I said to Alejandro
— who was like a commander —
that we ought to nail a patch on it.
                              No,
he says to me, I'm going right now to Sabino and either borrow
or steal his boat.
                    And then,
he says to me, I'd be willing to stay to fight the enemy;
as long as I had this M-50 they wouldn't lay a foot on this island,
but because of you and those children, we'd better get out of here.

EL ALCOHOLISMO

Estoy entre piedras y basuras
hediondas de mi pueblo.
Mi ropa está sucia y rota,
mis zapatos ya se terminaron.
Estoy de mal color y maloliente,
toda la gente me mira con desprecio.
Cuando estoy bien embriagado
canto y grito.
Mis hermanas moscas son mi compañía por el día
y los zancudos me chupan la sangre por la noche.

ANOCHE SOÑÉ

Anoche soñé con el San Juan de la Cruz
teníamos que transportar el montón de armas a Delicias
y allí enterrarlas;
teníamos que llevarlas por la mañana
porque el enemigo venía por la tarde.
El bote tenía dos hoyos grandes
y yo le decía a Alejandro
— que era como un comandante —
hay que clavarle tablas.
                              No,
me dice. Voy rápido donde Sabino a pedirle
o a robarle su bote.
                      Después,
me dice, yo me quedaría a combatir al enemigo,
con esta M-50 no entran en esta isla,
pero por ustedes, y esos niños, hay que irse.

I REMEMBER

I could never forget you, archipelago,
how after the rain would end
and the brilliant sun remained
Raúl would come by to take us to that farm named El Guabo
to pick oranges.
Under the dark green orange tree,
muddy puddles,
yellow oranges pricked by wasps,
cowshit
both fresh and dried,
and I up in the tree picking oranges,
Raúl gathering them, Nubia
tossing them into a sack, Lolo
taking them to the boat and Myriam
standing there sucking them.

GLORIA GUEVARA fought with great valor during the assault on San Carlos. She is a noted painter and works for the Nicaraguan government.

RECUERDO

No te podría olvidar archipiélago
cuando después que pasaba la lluvia
y quedaba el sol brillante
pasaba Raúl para llevarnos al guabo
a cortar naranjas.
Bajo los verdes oscuros naranjos,
lodazales,
naranjas amarillas picadas por avispas
miérdas de vaca
frescas y viejas.
Yo arriba del palo cortándolas,
Raúl cogiéndolas, la Nubia
echándolas al saco, Lolo
llevándolas al bote y la Myriam
chupándoselas.

IVÁN GUEVARA

AND SO THEY SENT YOU FAR AWAY FROM ME

And so they sent you far away
so you'd forget me
and perhaps someone else would take my place
but I know from what you gave me
you won't be able to forget me.
And the bathrobe you used is still there, still moist,
the smell of your perfume still clings to my clothes,
my lips still moist from the kiss you gave me that last time.
And as I weep I wonder when you'll be back:
I don't know if it will be by skiff or by launch,
all I know is someday you'll return.

RAILROAD WORK CREW

They're cutting oaks, guanacastes
cedars and laurels.
Way over there
at the bottom of a ravine
one leafy tree remains
and in its shadow, a pale deer.

Y TE MANDARON LEJOS DE MÍ

Y te mandaron lejos
para que te olvidaras de mí
y quizás otro ocupara mi lugar
pero sé que no me podrás olvidar por lo que me diste.
Y está allí el vestido de baño que vos usabas aún mojado,
mi ropa huele a los perfumes que vos usabas,
mis labios mojados por el beso que me diste por última vez.
Y mientras lloro me pregunto cuándo volverás,
no sé si en bote o en panga,
sólo sé que un día volverás.

COMPAÑÍA DEL TRÁNSITO

Cortan robles guanacastes
cedros y laureles.
A lo lejos
al fondo de una quebrada
ha quedado un árbol frondoso
y a su sombra, un venado pálido.

IT'S ALMOST NIGHT

It's almost night
and the lake is calm.
From time to time breezes stir.
The egrets head off to sleep.
The güises make a few last jumps.
But me, I'm alone
seeing off in the distance
the blue range of Chontales
and thinking
that at the edge of the lake
is the little village
where you are
Silvia.

AT THE FIESTA

As guitars were strumming in the background
without your realizing it I was watching you
and I started a conversation about the flower you were holding in
        your hand
and now with hands cold and trembling
both of us laugh to realize
that you too were searching the same as I.

ES CASI YA DE NOCHE

Es casi ya de noche y
el lago está calmo.
Brisas soplan de vez en cuando.
Las garzas pasan a dormir.
Los güises dan sus últimos saltos.
Pero yo estoy solo
viendo a lo lejos
las cordilleras azules de Chontales
y pienso
que a la orilla del lago
está el pequeño pueblo
donde estás vos
Silvia.

EN LA FIESTA

Cuando guitarras sonaban allá lejos
sin que vos te dieras cuenta yo te estaba viendo
y te hablé por la flor que tenías en tus manos
y ahora con las manos heladas y temblorosas
los dos nos reíamos al darnos cuenta
de que vos también buscabas lo mismo que yo.

WHAT I SAW ONE DAY BY THE LAKE

Above the peaks of Solentiname
a hawk drifts slowly by.
He leaves the mountains behind and flies out over the lake
swinging in circles and letting out long whistling cries
as though calling his prey. Suddenly there's the fish,
and the water has turned it all sorts of colors
        red-yellow   blue-silver
innocent to the very end. Seeing it, the wise hawk
hurls himself on the fish with his beak hard as ivory
and huge claws like steel hooks
and lifts the fish through the air.
The fish wiggles like a spring and manages to escape
but quickly the hawk drops back in pursuit
and nails him with even stronger talons
and there on a branch of a ceiba devours him.

NIGHT OF LOVE

That time we were fused by desire only the sound
of kisses broke the night
and in the next house a child was crying,
the wind made the flowers in the garden sway
and we stood there outside.
I kissed you again and again,
and you nervous but willing,
my hands curious, and you softly pushing them away,
and I saw the tears in your eyes I felt you mine that night
but then you went far away.
Now I have nothing but this memory you left me
and I think of the last word you spoke.

LO QUE YO VI UNA TARDE JUNTO AL LAGO

Sobre las montañas de Solentiname
un gavilán se pasea lentamente.
Deja las montañas y sigue volando sobre el lago
mientras baila y lanza largos silbidos
como llamando a su presa. De pronto aparece el pez
y el agua le hace verse de varios colores rojo-amarillo, azul-plateado,
inocente al fin. El inteligente gavilán al verlo
se lanza sobre él con su duro pico como de marfil
y grandes garras como garfios de acero y lo levanta por los aires.
El pez se sacude como un resorte y se logra zafar
pero rápido vuelve a cazar y le clava con más fuerza las uñas
y en una rama de una ceiba lo devora.

NOCHE DE AMOR

Cuando nos quisimos sólo el ruido de
los besos interrumpía la noche
y en la casa vecina un niño lloraba,
el viento mecía las flores del jardín
y nosotros parados allí afuera.
Yo te besaba una y otra vez
y vos nerivosa pero contenta;
mis manos curiosas, vos retirándolas suavemente
y te miré llorar te sentí mía esa noche
pero después te fuiste lejos.
Hoy sólo miro este recuerdo que me dejaste
y pienso en la última palabra que dijiste.

LOVE IS LIKE A BEAN PLANT

Have you seen the bean plant
grow? It's born, puts out
leaves, buds,
then flowers. And
later it only gives fruits and then
dry pods.
Well that's how love is.

TO MY NICARAGUA, FROM EXILE

Nicaragua, it weeps like a girl who's been abandoned,
Nicaragua weeps. But the day's not far off
when we'll no longer have to live underground or exiled
nor circulate clandestine documents or messages.
The day will come when up from the grave will rise thousands of heroes
as yet unknown to the people.
The day will come when we can shout in the open streets
LONG LIVE THE SANDINISTA FRONT.

EL AMOR ES COMO LA MATA DE FRIJOL

¿Has visto crecer la mata
de frijol? Nace, echa
hojas, chotes, florece. Y
después sólo da frutos y
vainas.
Pues así es el amor.

A MI NICARAGUA DESDE EL EXILIO

Nicaragua, llora Nicaragua como muchacha dejada,
llora Nicaragua. Pero no está lejos el día
en que ya no tengamos que vivir en la clandestinidad o el exilio
ni circulen papeletas y documentos clandestinos.
Llegará el día en que resuciten miles de héroes
aún ignorados por el pueblo.
Llegará el día en que podamos gritar en plena calle
VIVA EL FRENTE SANDINISTA.

IN SOLENTINAME

Everything was left behind there in Solentiname, the lake
the islands the church where we met every
Sunday, the avocado trees
near the plaza where we played soccer,
afternoons with the lake calm or slightly
rippled by the whipped fin of some shark
or a bathing güis, moonlit nights
when we played or danced with Nubia's
sisters, and I strummed my guitar, singing
some song or other by Silvio Rodríguez
or Carlos Mejía.
We'll never again see Ernesto come down
from his house to the wharf with his briefcase his cape
his hat and some book in his hand,
off to celebrate Mass at Papaturro.

YOU CAN HEAR SPEECHES LIKE THIS

They've all joined forces, Somoza's
Liberales and murderers.
Suddenly you hear the thump of contact bombs
bursts of machine gun fire, helicopters aloft,
people run by, terrified,
cries of women and children.
War! cry some old women.
Meanwhile, Somoza, nervous in his bulletproof bunker,
keeps on saying: "Just keep calm, folks,
everything's peaceful. I'll make sure there's law and order,
don't you worry. Here there's freedom and love."
But the jails are full of political prisoners,
and in the mountains peasant women are raped
by Somoza's Guardia,
kids have their throats cut, they're burned
in a heap with their fathers.
This is peace in Nicaragua.

108

EN SOLENTINAME

Todo quedó allá en Solentiname: el lago las
islas la iglesia donde nos reuníamos todos
los domingos, los árboles de aguacate que
están junto a la plaza donde jugábamos fútbol,
las tardes con el lago calmo o levemente
interrumpido por algún aletazo de un tiburón
o de un güis que se baña, las noches de luna
cuando jugábamos o bailábamos con las hermanas
de la Nubia, y mi guitarra con que tocaba y cantaba
algunas canciones de Silvio Rodríguez
o de Carlos Mejía.
Ya no volveremos a ver a Ernesto bajar de
su casa al muelle con el maletín su capote el
sombrero y algún libro en la mano para ir
a celebrar misa a Papaturro.

HAY DISCURSOS COMO ÉSTE

Están reunidos todos los liberales
y asesinos de Somoza.
De pronto se oyen estallidos de bombas de contacto
ráfagas de ametralladoras, helicópteros volando,
corre la gente despavorida
gritos de mujeres y niños.
¡La guerra! decían unas viejas.
Mientras, Somoza en una urna a prueba de bala,
nervioso, seguía hablando: "Calma pueblo
todo está en paz. Yo pondré el orden,
no tengan miedo. Aquí hay libertad, amor."
Pero las celdas están llenas de presos políticos,
en las montañas las mujeres campesinas son violadas
por la guardia de Somoza
los niños son degollados y quemados
junto con sus padres.
Esto es la paz de Nicaragua.

THE DESERTED CHURCH

The church stands empty and deserted now,
gone are the shouts of the children
the sound of guitars.
Now only nature pays it any mind.
The grass will reclaim it as before
wind and rain will lash the flowering palm
birds will come out to eat the mangos
swallows will go on building their nests
under the eaves of the church.
Now only flowers and the songs of birds
will gladden this place through the long silent days.

FOUR DAYS IN THE MOUNTAINS, THEN EXILE

How strange I feel in a country where I don't belong
and nobody knows me
and I have no place to go.
Escazú is the first place I recognize.
After the attack on the garrison
the one at the edge of the Great Lake
I slip into the mountains
crossing fields, slogging through mud
I enter the jungle which never refuses to hide the guerrillero
it its dense foliage
and so I go plodding farther and farther
leaving behind Nicaragua
with its bullet-riddled garrison
its guardsmen wounded
or finished off by guerrilla rifles.
The Nicaraguan Air Force flies over us like huge birds of prey
by now hundreds of guardsmen have been dropped off by choppers
to patrol the mountains like bloodhounds.
Now I go to the border marker
near the Rio Frío
and see the massive craters left by the bombs of the air force.

LA IGLESIA SOLA

Está sola la iglesia ahora
sin el grito de los niños
o el sonar de guitarras.
Ahora sólo la naturaleza da cuenta de eso.
Volverá a crecer la hierba como en un principio,
el viento y la lluvia azotarán la palmera florecida
llegarán los pájaros a comer mangos,
las golondrinas seguirán haciendo sus nidos
en los aleros de la iglesia.
Ahora sólo las flores y el canto de los pájaros
alegrarán allí en los días de silencio.

CUATRO DÍAS EN LA MONTAÑA Y EL EXILIO

Qué extraño me siento en un país al que no pertenezco
ni nadie me conoce.
Tampoco tengo adónde ir.
Escazú es el primer lugar que conozco.
Después del ataque al cuartelito
aquel que está a la orilla del Gran Lago
me introduje en la montaña
cruzando llanos, chapoteando lodo,
me interno entre la selva que nunca niega la espesura de la maleza
con la que oculta al guerrillero
y así voy caminando más y más
dejando atrás a Nicaragua
con su cuartelito acribillado a balazos,
guardias heridos
y muertos por los fusiles guerrilleros.
La FAN vuela sobre nosotros como inmensas aves da rapiña,
ya a esta hora cientos de guardias han sido bajados desde helicópteros
a las montañas para patrullar la zona como perros de cacería.
Voy pasando los mojones de la frontera
que están junto al río Frío
y veo los grandes huecos que dejara la FAN durante el bombardeo.

Hacienda "La Esperanza" where they murdered Dónald and Elvis
is only a couple kilometers from here.
I remember my brother [Dónald] when I saw him, sad, that
     next-to-last time,
and later I saw him at the dock where we parted
and I never saw him again.
We learned he'd been captured and killed along with my friend Elvis
and their cries at the hour of torture
were absorbed by the mountain.
After four days I arrive at Los Chiles
(home of the poet José Coronel Urtecho
who years ago was named my godfather in the church of Solentiname)
and it is here the Costa Rican Guardia Civil captured me.
Arrested, given medical care, then moved to the San José airport
I was interviewed by a beautiful woman
whose name I don't remember
only her eyes, large and yellow,
and I was filthy, covered with mud
but I still said nothing during the interview,
only promised to continue in the struggle of the FSLN.
How odd I feel there
all sorts of people keep watching me.
I feel like an animal captured in the wild
then brought down into the city.
Kept eight days by the Third Company
I'm allowed to live at Escazú
but I have to report to Immigration every day.
Carlos, the boss, always jokes with me.
One quite nice-looking girl gives me sidelong glances.
Ivonne stays serious when she watches me.
Rosa, dark with her hair in an afro, smiles and looks at me
but I can't tell if she's a little frightened
or just thinks I seem friendly.
Yanet, the religious one, looks at me as though she pities me.
My friend Benedicto congratulates me for the blows we've struck
     against Somoza.
Another girl I like, one who works with don Carlos,
never risked saying a word to me.
I hear the laugh of Andreína, the other tall black girl
whom I couldn't talk with because she'd only just arrived
(but as for me, after a while I stopped showing up because I went back
     to being a guerrillero).

112

La hacienda La Esperanza, donde asesinaron a Dónald y Elvis
está como a dos kilómetros de aquí.
Recuerdo a mi hermano cuando lo vi triste por penúltima vez,
después lo vi en el muelle donde nos separamos
y jamás lo volví a ver.
Supimos que lo capturaron y lo asesinaron junto a Elvis mi amigo
y sus gritos a la hora de la tortura
los absorbió la montaña.
Después de cuatro días llego a Los Chiles
(hacienda del poeta José Coronel Urtecho
que años atrás me lo dieran como padrino en la iglesia de Solentiname)
es aquí donde me capturó la guardia civil de Costa Rica.
Detenido, curado y trasladado al aeropuerto de San José
donde fui entrevistado por una mujer bonita
cuyo nombre no recuerdo,
sólo sus ojos, eran grandes y amarillos,
y yo sucio, lodoso todavía,
tampoco dije nada en la entrevista,
sólo prometí seguir en la lucha del FSLN.
Qué raro me siento
grupos de gente me quedan viendo.
Me siento como cuando un animal ha sido cogido vivo en la selva
y bajado a la ciudad.
Después de ocho días de estar preso en la Tercera Compañía
paso a vivir a Escazú
y tengo que ir diario a Migración.
Carlos, el jefe, me da cierta broma.
Una muchacha muy agradable me mira de reojo.
Ivonne permanece seria, mirándome.
Rosa, la morena de afro, sonríe y me mira,
pero no sé si es del susto o si es que le parezco amigable.
Yanet, la evangélica, me mira como sintiendo lástima por mí.
Benedicto, mi amigo, me saluda alegre por el golpe
que le dimos a Somoza.
Otra muchacha que me gusta y que trabaja con don Carlos
nunca se atrevió a decirme nada.
Oigo la risa de Andreína, la otra muchacha morena
alta que no pude hablarle porque era recién llegada
(y yo ya no seguí llegando porque me volví a la guerrilla).

FROM A HILLTOP
ON THE BENJAMÍN ZELEDÓN SOUTHERN FRONT

And I'm here in my trench
camouflaged with freshly cut grass.
The 20 compañeros I have with me on this hill
are all in their trenches
in position ready on the lookout.
The "suck 'n' blow" zips past,
farther off a D43 reconnaissance plane.
And you can hear mortars all around us,
cannons and mortars, 120s and 82s.
The planes let go with bursts of 50-calibre machine gun fire.
The "push-and-pull" in a zigzag dive
strafing the hillsides
hitting Peñas Blancas and Sapoá with rocket fire,
the chopper that hovers up there
and drops 500-pound bombs,
bombs supplied by the North American government
for killing our people.
We're all hungry,
three days without food, and the condensed milk
and tuna that got through doesn't amount to much,
our hair's all in tangles,
our faces dirty, we've been wearing these clothes
for eight days straight.
The afternoon here has been fairly calm,
we guerrilleros are hidden in the underbrush, waiting.
The high hill. My view commands the entire valley
and I can see the rooftops of all the houses
in Sapoá and Peñas Blancas.
The colors of the rooftiles strike me as being
like those the sun makes setting.
My FAL is ready and loaded, pointing straight ahead,
there are hundreds of Somoza's "Chigüines"
all over this area.
On the radio I hear the voice of María the radio operator
and of Leonardo the artilleryman (they're on another hill)
Leonardo who came here to meet me
at the urging of María
she who is today my close friend.

DESDE UNA COLINA
EN EL FRENTE SUR BENJAMÍN ZELEDÓN

Y estoy aquí en mi trinchera
camuflado con zacate recién cortado.
Los veinte compañeros que tengo yo en la colina
todos están en sus trincheras
apostados vigilando atentos.
El "chupi-sopla" pasa veloz,
más atrás un avión de reconocimiento un D43.
Y se oyen morteros por todos lados
cañonazos y morteros de 120 y 82.
Los aviones dejan ir ráfagas de ametralladoras calibre 50.
El "push-and-pull" zigzagueando en picada
ametrallando las colinas
roqueteando a Peñas Blancas y Sapoá,
el helicóptero que se para allá arriba
y deja caer bombas de 500 libras,
bombas que suministraba el gobierno de Norte América
para matar la población.
Hay hambre en todos nosotros
son tres días sin comer y la leche condensada
y el atún que nos ha llegado es muy poco,
nuestros pelos todos desgreñados,
la cara sucia, nuestra ropa ya tiene ocho días
de estar con nosotros.
La tarde ha sido aparentemente calma,
los guerrilleros estamos ocultos
dentro de la maleza, esperando.
La colina alta. Domino todo el valle
y veo el techo de todas las casas
de Sapoá y Peñas Blancas.
Los colores de los techos se me parecen
a los que hizo el sol al ocultarse.
Mi FAL está bala en boca apuntando hacia adelante
pues son cientos de chigüines los que hay
en toda la faja territorial.
Por la radio oigo hablar de María la radio-operadora
de Leonardo el artillero (que están en otra colina)
Leonardo que vino aquí a conocerme
por indicaciones de María
la que hoy es mi amiga.

IN THE GUERRILLA CAMP

It has stopped raining here on the mountain
but the trees still drip the last drops of water
the partridge sings "tac tac"
and the dark green of the forest
makes the color of that canary
stand out yellow.

A QUIET MOMENT

The silence brought me memories
of that girl called
Raquel, because after all that's happened
there's nothing left me but nostalgia.

AFTER THE AMBUSH

The darkness comes in fast, it starts to rain and
the footprints of the guerrilleros are washed away.
We're wasted with fatigue;
the plain we have to cross is wide,
the mud and water come up to our belts
and now at last it's total dark, not a single star in the sky;
the column slogs on in silence.
Only one guerrillero thinks of writing a poem.
It goes on raining, the mosquitos rise up from the jupati palms,
the hunger and the pull of sleep are intense.
If I lean back I'm spiked by thorns that make my body ache and swell.
No sound of gunfire,
we're not far from camp;
the order comes to take five. One of the compañeros,
smoking a cigarette, asks me:
"Are you really a poet?"

EN EL CAMPAMENTO GUERRILLERO

Ha dejado de llover aquí en la montaña.
Todavía los árboles dejan caer las últimas gotas de agua
tac tac cantó una codorniz
y el verde oscuro de la selva
resalta el color de aquel
canario amarillo.

EN MOMENTO DE SILENCIO

El silencio me trajo los recuerdos
de aquella muchacha que le llaman
Raquel, porque después de todo lo pasado
sólo me queda la nostalgia.

DESPUÉS DE LA EMBOSCADA

Oscurece pronto, comienza a llover y
se borran las pisadas de los guerrilleros.
Hay cansancio en nosotros;
el llano que hay que pasar es grande,
el lodo y el agua nos llegan a la cintura
y ahora todo está oscuro, ni una estrella se ve en el cielo;
la columna camina en silencio.
Sólo un guerrillero piensa escribir un poema.
Sigue lloviendo, los zancudos salen de las yolillas,
el hambre y el sueño es intenso. Me arrecuesto y se
me clavan espinas que entumen mi cuerpo.
No se oyen disparos,
estamos ya cerca del campamento;
se da la orden de descanso. Un compañero,
mientras se fuma un cigarro, me pregunta:
¿es cierto que vos sos poeta?

DAWN WATCH

Five in the morning. The forest is still dark,
all the guerrilleros are asleep,
only we who have watch duty are awake.
The howler monkeys begin to croon throughout the forest.
My compañeros begin to rise with great enthusiasm
joining the birds.
I with my rifle frozen between my hands.

ON THE MOUNTAIN

The wind blows here on the mountain
where we guerrilleros have made camp near a river;
its water flows and flows,
it flows off to distant places yet there's always water here in the river.
The road can't tell the Gurditas
where we came from, where we're going.
Mountain, you who have seen us sleeping on your soil
at the foot of a tree on the side of a hill
but who also have your law
according to the legend of Chief Nicarao;
Mountain, guard our clandestinity
and our secrets of war.

UNA POSTA AL AMANECER

Las cinco de la mañana. La selva está oscura todavía,
todos los guerrilleros están dormidos
sólo los que hacen postas estamos despiertos.
Los congos comienzan a cantar por toda la selva.
Mis compañeros comienzan a levantarse con gran entusiasmo
junto con los pájaros.
Yo con el fusil helado entre mis manos.

EN LA MONTAÑA

El viento sopla aquí en la montaña
donde los guerrilleros hacemos un campamento junto a un río,
su agua corre más y más
se va lejos y sin embargo siempre hay agua aquí en el río.
El camino que no puede decirle a los guarditas
de dónde venimos ni hacia dónde vamos;
montaña, vos que nos has visto dormir en el suelo
al pie de un árbol a la falda de un cerro
pero vos también tenés tu ley
según cuenta la leyenda del cacique Nicarao;
montaña, guardá nuestro clandestinaje
y nuestros secretos de guerra.

POEM TO A GIRL

For many days I have thought of writing this poem
and you more than anyone will know that I wrote it only for you
for the tall girl white girl with long copper-colored hair
small face blue eyes and tiny mouth.
I have decided not to put your name in the poem
partly to keep folks guessing and partly to foster illusions
in some other girls who look like the one I describe.
When somewhere in California you read this poem
you will remember me, if you haven't erased me
from your memory yet.
And while there is nothing possible between us now
at least we had the good luck to be together for a while
thus outflanking my rivals;
keep to yourself this fond memory
if in fact you understood
what one day long ago
a poet tried
to tell you.

WHEN YOU SEE THIS POEM

It's not that I'm fishing for your love with this poem
only that I want to trick your lips into smiling
because whatever movement you make at this very moment
that'll be your answer
and if I fail to provoke even a single blink of your eyes,
right now, while this may be happening or not there in the city,
here in the mountains a guerrilla troop
is drilling for the fight against Somoza's Guardia;
and you, Silvia, will be inside me
at the hour of combat.

POEMA A UNA MUCHACHA

Desde hace días había pensado escribir este poema
y vos mejor que nadie sabrás que lo hice sólo para vos
a la muchacha alta, blanca, pelo largo y rojizo
cara pequeña ojos azules y boca chiquita.
He decidido no poner tu nombre en el poema
para curiosidad de la gente y para ilusión
de algunas otras muchachas similares a la que yo describo.
Cuando en algún lugar de California leás este poema
me recordarás, si es que aún no me has borrado
de tus recuerdos.
Y si ya no es posible nada
pero los dos tuvimos la suerte de haber estado juntos
desafiando así a mis rivales,
guardá vos sola hoy la nostalgia
si es que entendiste
lo que un día
te quiso decir
un poeta.

CUANDO VEAS ESTE POEMA

No es que yo pretenda tu amor con este poema
sino tan sólo provocar una sonrisa en tus labios
porque cualquier movimiento que hagás en este momento
será tu respuesta
y si no logro provocar ni un solo parpadeo en tus ojos
entonces, mientras esto ocurra o no allá en la ciudad
aquí en las montañas un campamento guerrillero
se entrena para luchar contra la guardia de Somoza;
y vos, Silvia, estarás en mí
a la hora del combate.

FORGOTTEN LOVE

Without wanting to I find myself thinking
that the great love I felt yesterday
for that girl I will someday
forget.

SUNDAY MORNING IN THE GARRISON

I had never felt it before
until today Sunday morning
December 16th.
At the very moment that I was quietly reading
How to be a Young Communist
by Ernesto Che Guevara
at that moment a radio, the volume fairly low,
let loose a love song
which somehow filled the command post.
And suddenly without knowing why I thought of you, Jilma:
Why are you my friend? I don't know.
Why do I like you? I don't know,
perhaps I'll never know,
and this poem will become nothing more than a memory
for me and for you in the future.

IVÁN GUEVARA fought at San Carlos and later until the triumph in 1979. He is presently an officer in the Nicaraguan Army and lives in Managua. He still writes poetry and publishes in magazines.

AMOR OLVIDADO

Sin querer estoy pensando
que el gran amor que ayer tenía
por esa muchacha un día lo
olvidaré.

DOMINGO POR LA MAÑANA EN EL CUARTEL

Nunca lo había sentido antes
sino hasta hoy domingo por la mañana
16 de diciembre.
En el momento en que leía en silencio
el escrito *Cómo Debe Ser Un Joven Comunista*
de Ernesto Che Guevara,
en ese momento un radio con bajo volumen
dejaba oir una canción de amor
que llenaba el comando.
Y de pronto sin saber por qué pensé en vos Jilma
¿Por qué sos mi amiga? No lo sé
¿Por qué me gustás? Tampoco lo sé
tal vez nunca lo sabré,
y este poema venga a ser nada más un recuerdo
para mí y para vos en el futuro.

PEDRO PABLO MENESES

THE RED MALINCHE

The red malinche
the yellow-flowering "Cortés de la Cigüeña"
the tortoises lumbering up to lay their eggs under the full moon.
The pocoyos sing
the fields burnt
the deer drinking water on the dry shore.
The first rains have arrived
smell of the moist earth, the güises sing happily
it's May in Solentiname.

NIGHT

Night with a full moon
reflected in the calm lake;
the lake gilded and silvered.
I see a cormorant
hunting sardines.
A chorus of toads singing.
And the joyful song of the pocoyos,
They're saying: Jodido! Rejodido!
hopping from stone to stone.
The owl goes by whistling.
A cool wind blows.

APRIL

I remember that April night
you and I under a full moon
unaware of our presence.
The full moon rises and sets again,
another summer will come and go
but you're not here.

EL MALINCHE ROJO

El malinche rojo
el cortés de la cigüeña florecido amarillo,
las tortugas subiendo a desovar en noche de luna llena.
Cantan los pocoyos,
los llanos quemados,
los venados bebiendo agua en la costa seca.
Han llegado las primeras lluvias,
olor a tierra mojada, los güises cantan alegres,
es mayo en Solentiname.

NOCHE

La noche con una luna llena
reflejada en el lago calmo;
el lago dorado y plateado.
Veo un cuaco
cazando sardinas.
Un coro de sapos cantando.
El alegre canto de los pocoyos
diciendo: Jodido, rejodido
brincando de una piedra a otra.
La lechuza pasa silbando.
Sopla un viento fresco.

ABRIL

Recuerdo la noche de abril
con una luna llena
inocente de nosotros dos.
La luna llena vuelve a pasar,
otro verano pasará
per vos no estás.

MALINCHE

The bright red malinche, the dazzling sand along the shore
where the tortoises come up to lay eggs. The yellow-flowering
"Cortés de La Cigüeña" and a flock of ducks flies by
across the sunset; standing on doña Olivia's stony beach
an egret staring at his white reflection in the water.

RIPE MANGOS

Ripe mangos, helequemes,
maderos, sonsonates,
all in flower,
flocks of chocoyos,
yellow-tufted parrots,
grackles,
all in a mango tree, singing.
Doña Olivia's house reflected in the lake,
don Julio Guevara with his fishing pole,
the boat seems to be cutting glass,
its string of red mojarras,
palometas, guapotes and croakers.
Don Julio knows in what cave to find armadillos
and where there are garrobos.

IN NICARAGUA THE GREAT ASSAULT

In Nicaragua the great assault on the garrison of San Carlos
that cold dawn.
On the 12th I looked out from the stronghold toward Solentiname.
The Rio San Juan flowing past full of clumps of floating grass
and beach hens,
ducks travelling on a log downriver.
Time passes like a shooting star.
We are going toward final victory.
We will be free or be martyrs.

EL MALINCHE

El malinche colorado, la arena brillante de la costa
donde las tortugas suben a desovar. El amarillo cortés
de la cigüeña florecido y una bandada de patos va volando
en una puesta de sol, en el cascajo de doña Olivia
una garza mirando su reflejo blanco en el agua.

MANGOS MADUROS

Mangos maduros, helequemes,
maderos, sonsonates,
todos florecidos,
manadas de chocoyos,
loros copete amarillo,
clarineros,
todos en un palo de mango cantando.
La casa de doña Olivia reflejada en el lago,
don Julio Guevara con su vara de pescar,
el bote parece cortar vidrio,
su sarta de mojarras rojas,
palometas y guapotes, roncadores.
Don Julio sabe en qué cueva hay cusucos
y dondé hay garrobos.

EN NICARAGUA EL GRAN ASALTO

En Nicaragua el gran asalto al cuartel de San Carlos
aquella madruga fría.
El 12 desde la fortaleza miré Solentiname.
El río San Juan corriendo con gamalotes y gallinas
de playa, los patos viajando en una tuca río abajo.
El tiempo pasa como una estrella fugaz.
Iremos hasta la victoria final.
Seremos libres o seremos mártires.

ALL DAY CARS GO BY

All day cars go by
fouling the air.
The mountain, full of fresh cool air,
small birds sing at dusk,
the river flowing by.
I remember my Solentiname with its calm lake
and the zanates flying on toward the tall grass.
But one day I'll return to a Nicaragua without Tacho.
I am living in exile.

COOL MORNING

Cool morning. The sun comes in
my blue window. The song of the güis
in the fig tree.
I remember Dónald in San Miguel
strolling down those streets by moonlight
holding hands with his girl
for the last time that Saturday.
In October, that night in San Carlos
you two fought
side by side with me.
Today you're in jail.

TODO EL DÍA PASAN AUTOS

Todo el día pasan autos
contaminando el aire.
La montaña llena de aire fresco,
pequeños pájaros cantan al atardecer,
el río corriendo.
Recuerdo mi Solentiname con el lago calmo
y los zanates pasando hacia aquel zacatón.
Pero un día regresaré sin Tacho en Nicaragua.
Estoy viviendo en el exilio.

LA MAÑANA FRESCA

La mañana fresca. El sol entra
por mi ventana celeste. El canto del güis
en el chilamate.
Recuerdo a Dónald en San Miguel
por aquellas calles en noche de luna,
de la mano con su novia
por último aquel sábado.
En octubre ustedes combatieron
junto a mí
en aquella noche en San Carlos.
Hoy están presos.

YOUR LONG HAIR

With your long black hair, your
faded jeans
and your blue coat, with your rollerskates
over your shoulder, you got off
the San Pedro bus.
Girl, though I may never know
your name, I still write you
these verses.

SAN MIGUEL

San Miguel I remember you for the girl
who came every night to my room.
Carolina you appear in my dreams to visit me;
when I wake, only emptiness remains.
Carolina, I remember you, Carolina.

THE EVENING IS COOL

The evening is cool
with red and rose and yellow clouds
tinted by the sun hiding itself
behind the mountain.
You and I, girl,
hand in hand in Solentiname.
Now evening appears
with clouds and the sun hiding
behind Irazú volcano,
you in Solentiname
and I in exile.

TU PELO LARGO

Tu pelo largo y negro, con tu
blue-jeans descolorido,
y tu abrigo azul con tus patines
en la espalda, te bajaste
del bus de San Pedro.
Muchacha aunque tu nombre
nunca lo sepa, a vos te escribo
estos versos.

SAN MIGUEL

San Miguel te recuerdo por una muchacha
en cada noche en mi cuarto.
Carolina vos llegás en sueños a visitarme,
cuando me despierto, sólo el vacío queda.
Carolina, te recuerdo, Carolina.

LA TARDE ESTÁ FRESCA

La tarde está fresca
con nubes rojas, rosadas y amarillas
por el reflejo del sol acultándose
detrás de la montaña.
Vos y yo, muchacha
agarrados de la mano en Solentiname.
Hoy la tarde se parece
con las nubes y el sol ocultándose detrás
del volcán Irazú,
vos en Solentiname
y yo en el exilio.

THE MOON RISING

The moon rising from behind the hill,
an owl sitting in a peach tree
hoots and flies off,
the neighboring dogs begin to howl,
and off in the distance
other dogs.

THE NIGHT COLD

The night cold,
moon in the sky.
Toads singing to
their ladies.
In the street a couple saying goodbye
at a bus stop,
but you're not here.

GUERRILLA RECONNAISSANCE

The golden-yellow corteses on cattle ranches
There will be schools there
the helequemes in the fertile plain of the crystalline river
in the pool the guapote moving its brightly colored little fins
blowing bubbles out of his mouth, they float straight up
the white-flowered laurel and the patacona doves, feet
and beak red, their eyes scarlet as blood.

132

LA LUNA SALIENDO

La luna saliendo tras el cerro,
en el palo de durazno una lechuza sentada,
se levanta chiflando y se aleja,
en el vecindario aúllan los perros
y más lejos
otros perros.

LA NOCHE FRÍA

La noche fría,
el cielo con luna.
Los sapos cantando
a sus hembras.
En la calle una pareja despidiéndose
en una parada de bus,
pero vos no estás.

RECONOCIMIENTO GUERRILLERO

Los corteses amarillo-dorado en los potreros de ganado
allí serán escuelas
los helequemes rojos en la vega del río cristalino
en la poza el guapote moviendo las alitas pinto todito
echando popas por la boca que salen arriba
el laurel florecido blanco y palomas pataconas, patas
y pico rojo, el ojo púrpura como sangre.

FOGGY MOUNTAIN

Foggy mountain, cold, shafts of sunlight glimmer
through the green foliage, the song of the chorchas
    "Chorchita, chorchita"
the toucan red breast yellow beak
and the guás in the dry tree announcing summer.
My liberating rifle and I frozen in place, waiting in the tall grass,
and the National Guard, like the jaguar, waits for the tapir.

PEDRO PABLO MENESES, characterized by his former friends as "an in-
decisive kid," and "naïve when it came to ideology," fought during the San
Carlos assault, but left Solentiname in the early '80s to join former San-
dinista/then contra Eden Pastora and his ARDE forces in Costa Rica. Pedro
Pablo died in suspicious circumstances not long after he arrived in Costa Rica;
rumor has it that ARDE thought he was a spy and killed him.

LA MONTAÑA NEBLINOSA

La montaña neblinosa, fría, los rayos del sol rielan
tras el follaje verde, el canto de las chorchas chorchita chorchita
el tucán pecho rojo pico amarillo
y el guas en palo seco anunciando verano.
Mi fusil libertario como yo helado esperando en los pajonales
y la Guardia Nacional como el tigre espera al danto.

ALEJANDRO GUEVARA

THE EGRETS

The large egrets
white and elegant
fishing all day.
They squawk at each other and even do battle when some other bird
fishes in their favorite shallows.
Every sardine means a trip to the nest
because in that narrow stomach
there's only room for two fish —
one for herself
another, food for her fledgling.

From a distance you could mistake
an egret for a Virgin.

ALEJANDRO GUEVARA, a veteran of both the Gospel discussions and the assault on the National Guard garrison, is governor of the San Carlos region and a deputy in the National Assembly. He is married to Nubia Arcia.

LAS GARZAS

Las garzas grandes
blancas y elegantes
pescando todo el día.
Protestan y hasta pelean cuando otra
pesca en su costa favorita.
Cada sardina es un viaje al nido
porque en su estrecho estómago
caben dos
una de su alimento y otra para
un pichón.

Una garza de largo
se puede confundir con una virgen.

NUBIA ARCIA

WITH MY HAIR LOOSE

With my hair shook loose
blouse open, barefoot
I lie back on this boulder covered with moss
and swallow droppings.
And with eyes fixed on the moon
through the branches of the oak
I think of you, Alejandro.

I REMEMBER THAT DAWN

I remember that October dawn
when we were fleeing the National Guard
after the assault on the San Carlos garrison
and I started to drown crossing the Rio Frío
and I cried: Iván! I'm drowning!"

But it was not Iván who got to me first —
it was you, Alejandro.

CON EL PELO ALBOROTADO

Con el pelo alborotado
la blusa abierta y los pies descalzos
estoy acostada sobre una piedra curtida de lama
y mierda de golondrinas.
Y con los ojos fijos mirando la luna a través
de las ramas del roble, pienso en vos Alejandro.

RECUERDO AQUELLA MADRUGADA

Recuerdo aquella madrugada de octubre
cuando huíamos de la Guardia Nacional
después del asalto al cuartel de San Carlos
cuando me ahogaba al cruzar el río Frío
y grité: — Me ahogo Iván.

Pero no fue Iván el primero en llegar
sino que fuiste vos Alejandro.

LETTER

I am in this room
it is night it is raining.
I have stayed here playing on the bed with my daughter, Alejandra.
Before my eyes the lantern glows.
I see a photo of Sandino
and next to it a cartridge clip from a Garand and it's full
and there's also the hollow shell of a grenade
and under it a hundred-colones bill
and in the little hole at the top, a flower.
Alejandro, I hold in my hands the letter you sent
to the Agudelos in Colombia
in which you tell them of your guerrilla life,
you write: "From where I am I can see Solentiname,
La Zanata, Ometepe, and on a clear day as far as the cordillera
of Chontales where we used to go by launch.
Sometimes I strip and plunge into the lake;
sometimes we eat guapotes, mojarras, iguanas, tortoises.
Now that it's summer there are thousands of little ticks.
Sometimes just when I'm most relaxed
maybe I'll be eating some tasty chunk of grilled meat
and in zooms the air force
blasting away with tracer rockets."

SEATED IN THE GARDEN

Seated in the garden
Alejandra plays with a flower
she looks at it, sucks it, and laughs.

CARTA

Estoy en el cuarto
es de noche y está lloviendo.
Me he quedado jugando con mi hija Alejandra sobre la cama.
Enfrente tengo una lámpara prendida.
Veo una foto de Sandino
y a su lado un clip de Garand y está cargado,
también hay una granada desactivada,
debajo de ella un billete de cien colones
y en el huequito de arriba hay una flor.
Alejandro, en mis manos tengo la carta que le enviaste
a los Agudelo a Colombia
donde les cuentas tu vida en la guerrilla
y les dices: de donde estoy puedo ver Solentiname
La Zanata, Ometepe y cuando está despejado hasta la cordillera
de Chontales donde pasábamos en el lanchón.
Hay veces desnudo me doy mi chapuzón en el lago
también comemos guapotes, mojarras, iguanas y tortugas.
Ahora que es verano hay miles de garrapatitas.
A veces cuando más tranquilo estoy
tal vez con buena hambre comiéndome un lomo asado
viene la aviación con rastreo-roket.

SENTADA EN EL JARDÍN

Sentada en el jardín
Alejandra juega con una flor
la mira, la chupa y se ríe.

IT'S A BEAUTIFUL AFTERNOON

It's a beautiful afternoon
not too hot.
On the other side of the patio in front of my house
I see a fat old black woman
and some kids in shorts
and an old man in palmfrond hat
who plants seeds in this land
given them by the Revolution.

NUBIA ARCIA lives on Isla Felipe Peña in Solentiname where she paints, raises her children and manages a large woodworking cooperative. She is married to Alejandro Guevara. She took part in the assault on San Carlos, and still keeps the hollowed-out hand grenade mentioned in "Letter," occasionally using it to hold flowers.

142

HACE UNA TARDE HERMOSA

Hace una tarde hermosa
el calor es poco.
Al otro lado del patio de mi casa
veo una vieja gorda morena
y unos niños de pantalón corto;
un viejo con sombrero de palma
que siembra la tierra que les ha dado la Revolución.

WILLIAM GUEVARA

FISH

They play in the water submerging themselves they are variously
colored some are quite showy and they come in various sizes they feed
on sardines. God said: I will make them aquatic so they'll live in the
water just as people live on dry land.
They are as old as the wind.

BY FIRELIGHT

It is Holy Week when the rivers dry up
when the earth grows parched.
The birds of Solentiname stunned by the heat
sit in the trees or fly toward the water.
Always on the lookout for the animals that prowl the beach
they splash their wings and sing for joy.
At night the moon reflects itself in the clear waters.
I am here on these sands watching the moon
and enjoying the Southwind and Northwind
that struggle one against the other.

MOONLIT NIGHT

When the light of the sun has hidden itself behind the green mountain
it's then the egrets go by.
They fly in groups toward their nests.
That's when the moonbeams come out.
The faces of the stars peek out at us
as the pocoyos sing.
The moon watches herself within the waters.
She almost seems to be combing her yellow hair.

WILLIAM GUEVARA, one of the youngest of the Guevara kids, is studying in
Cuba.

LOS PECES

Juegan en el agua sumergiéndose tienen varios colores
algunos son vistosos también tienen varios tamaños se
alimentan de sardinas. Dios dijo los voy a hacer acuáticos
que vivan en las aguas como las personas viven en la tierra.
Tienen la misma edad del viento.

A LA LUZ DE LA FOGATA

Es la Samana Santa cuando los ríos se secan
cuando la tierra se reseca.
Los pájaros de Solentiname aturdidos por el calor
se sientan en los árboles y vuelan en dirección al agua.
Siempre con miedo a los animales de la playa
se empapan sus alas y cantan alegres.
En la noche la luna se ilumina en las claras aguas.
Yo en las arenas viendo la luna
y disfrutando de las brisas del Sur y Norte
que se pelean.

NOCHE DE LUNA

Cuando la luz del sol se ha ocultado entre las verdes montañas
es entonces cuando las garzas pasan.
En grupos van volando en dirección a sus nidos.
Es cuando se miran los rayos de la luna.
Las estrellas asoman sus caras
cuando los pocoyos cantan.
La luna se mira entre las aguas.
Pareciera peinarse sus cabellos amarillos.

ESPERANZA GUEVARA

HERE IN THIS LITTLE COVE

Here in this little cove
where there's a genízaro tree
full grown
full of branches
and mountain hens
sometimes with flowers and songbirds
surrounded by zacate and sontole
here is where
I meet Ernesto.

SUMMER

March and April
summer season
that time of year.
Only in summer can you
burn over the dried pasture land
and the cut brush
and only then
do the cicadas come out
and you bring home more fish
than venison.

YESTERDAY I WENT PAST THIS LITTLE FARM

The little farm was filthy
because it was still too soon;
the kids were dirty
because it was still too soon
and in the old crumpled album
was a photo of Somoza
because it was still too soon.

ESPERANZA GUEVARA is a well-known painter and lives in San Carlos with
her husband, Bosco Centeno.

146

EN ESTA ENSENADA

En esta ensenada
donde está un genízaro
muy bien crecido
todo lleno de ramas
y gallinitas de monte
a veces con flores y pájaros
rodeado de zacatillos y sontoles
aquí es donde encuentro
a Ernesto.

VERANO

Marzo y abril
temporada de verano
una estación del año.
Sólo en el verano es cuando se pueden
quemar potreros
y desmontes
y sólo entonces
es cuando salen las chicharras
y es mayor la caza de pescados
que de venados.

AYER PASÉ POR ESTE RANCHITO

El ranchito estaba sucio
porque es muy temprano;
los niños estaban sucios
porque es muy temprano
y en el forrito viejo y destartalado
estaba una foto de Somoza
porque es muy temprano.

MYRIAM GUEVARA

ALL MORNING IT HAS RAINED

All morning it has rained.
Two in the afternoon.
The lake has stayed calm.
Adán's launch goes by:
some are under the awning,
others stand in the stern.
Between the islands of La Palometa
and La Atravesada comes another launch
yellow, with a red bow.
As it comes into the rocky lagoon
up rises a flock of ducks.

FEBRUARY AFTERNOON

The sun is clear now
some swallows
fly around and around the church
a breeze moves the leaves of the trees
which surround it
from the shore I hear
the trumpeting song of a clarinero.

GUAVAS

The bluish-green ones
are too young.
Pure green they're ready to pick.
And the ripe ones
yellow, with pink insides.
When you move the branch
black wasps fly up
leaving behind ripe fruit
pricked full of holes.

TODA LA MAÑANA HA LLOVIDO

Toda la mañana ha llovido.
Las 2 de la tarde.
El lago ha quedado calmo.
Pasa la lanchita de Adán:
unos en la tolda
y otros de pie en la popa.
En medio de las islas La Palometa
y La Atravesada, viene otra lancha,
amarilla y las amuras en rojo.
Al pasar por el corral de piedras
se levanta una bandada de patos.

UNA TARDE DE FEBRERO

El sol está despejado
algunas golondrinas
vuelan alrededor de la iglesia
una brisa mueve las hojas de los árboles
que la rodean
desde la costa oigo
un clarinero cantar.

LAS GUAYABAS

Las verde-azul
son tiernas.
Las sazonas verde claro.
Y las maduras
amarillas, y rosado por dentro.
Al mover la rama,
se levantan avispas negras
dejando las maduras picadas.

THAT NIGHT

That Sunday night
when you came
I had planned
to tell you we were through.
But then it was
Monday morning.
Yellow shirt,
blue jeans
your tape recorder and a satchel
in your hands,
step by step
you walked slowly away.

AFTER THE BATTLE

It's six in the evening.
I feel feverish.
It starts to rain in
big continuous drops.
I cut two leaves
green and round
and put them on my head.
Nearby we can see
the lights of Los Chiles.

FUE AQUELLA NOCHE

Fue aquella noche de domingo
que viniste
cuando pensaba
decirte que termináramos.
Pero fue lunes
por la mañana.
Una camiseta amarilla
y de bluyín,
la grabadora y un maletín
en las manos.
Te marchaste
lentamente paso por paso.

DESPUÉS DEL COMBATE

Son las seis de la tarde.
Me siento con fiebre.
Comienza a llover en
gotas grandes y seguidas.
Corto dos hojas
verdes y redondas
las pongo en mi cabeza.
Cerca de nosotros
se ven las luces de Los Chiles.

TO CHATO MEDRANO, WHO FELL
DURING THE ASSAULT ON THE GARRISON OF SAN CARLOS

That October dawn
dressed in blue jeans and bright blue jacket
assault gun in your hand
you fought side by side with us.
Entering the old garrison
you were wounded in the right leg;
half dragging yourself and with the help of a compañero
you made it back to us,
your face broad and calm but pale,
shouting: "Hold your positions!"

ON THE BUS

On the bus
a girl
standing with a
bunch of flowers.
I remember you
that afternoon
coming by way of the post office
buying a
bunch of red flowers
for me.

MYRIAM GUEVARA, one of the best of the Solentiname painters, now lives
with her mother doña Olivia in Managua. She fought during the assault on
San Carlos.

AL CHATO MEDRANO,
CAÍDO EN EL ASALTO AL CUARTEL DE SAN CARLOS

En aquella madrugada de octubre
de bluyín y chaqueta de azulón
con escopeta de asalto
combatiste junto a nosotros.
Al entrar al viejo cuartel
te hirieron en la pierna derecha;
arrastrándote y con ayuda de un compañero
llegaste hasta nosotros.
Tu cara amplia pero pálida
gritando: — Guarden sus posiciones.

EN EL BUS

En el bus
una muchacha
de pie con un
ramo de flores.
Te recuerdo
aquella tarde
viniendo por el correo
comprando un
ramo de flores
rojas para me.

NATALIA SEQUEIRA

WHEN THE SUMMER MOONS GROW BRIGHT

When the summer moons grow bright
and there is moonlight beneath the trees
that is when the gathered pocoyos
hop and sing and fall in love.
The females make nests of dry leaves
and lay their eggs
when the moon slips behind the mountain.
The pocoyos disperse here and there
each from his perch, her perch, crying:
"Rejodido!" "Caballero!" "Corcobejo!"
as long as the dark night lingers.

IT WAS A NIGHT OF TORMENT

It was a night of torment.
I went out to the patio in search of peace.
I thought I would die.
I sought air but found none.
I retired to a madero tree,
there I doubted my sanity.
After the minutes of anguish were over
I sat on a stone
until the sun's rays
announced the dawn.

CUANDO LAS LUNAS VERANERAS ALUMBRAN

Cuando las lunas veraneras alumbran
bajo los árboles
es cuando los pocoyos reunidos
brincan cantan enamorados.
Las hembras hacen los nidos de hojas secas
y ponen sus huevos
cuando la luna se pierde tras la montaña.
Los pocoyos se alejan
cada quien por su lado gritando:
rejodido – caballero – corcobejo
quedando la noche oscura.

LA NOCHE FUE DE MARTIRIO

La noche fue de martirio.
Salí al patio buscando tranquilidad.
Sentí que me moría.
Buscaba aire y no lo encontraba.
Me arrecosté a un árbol de madero
allí no supe de mi juicio.
Pasados los minutos de angustia
en una piedra me senté
hasta que los rayos solares
anunciaban el amanecer.

THE BIRDS GO ABOUT BOUND TOGETHER BY LOVE

The birds go about bound together by love
searching for food in February.
The trees all lose their leaves,
the birds sit on bare branches
and feel unhapy,
they have nowhere among the leaves
to search for caterpillars and bugs to eat.
When May comes in they rejoice and open their wings,
greet each other, sing and stretch their necks,
seeing the trees now thick with leaves.

HUMMINGBIRDS FEEL LOVE

Hummingbirds feel love for their chicks
just as a mother might feel for her children.
It is seven in the morning
and they have been unable to feed their broods:
this is when they fly like crazy from garden to garden
seeking nectar from flowers,
and when it's been found, they speed like arrows
back to the nest.
The young wait for the mother's return
then open their beaks;
she proceeds to give them their breakfast.

THE CURLEW

The curlew sings at six in the morning
and goes on singing all day —
he tells the hour like a clock.

TODOS LOS PÁJAROS ANDAN EN UN CONJUNTO DE AMOR

Todos los pájaros andan en un conjunto de amor
buscando comida en febrero.
Todos los árboles botan las hojas,
los pájaros se sientan en las ramas
y se sienten tristes,
no tienen dónde buscar sus gusanos y otros animales
entre las hojas, para alimentarse.
Cuando entra mayo se alegran y abren sus alas,
se saludan, cantan y estiran el pescuezo
mirando los árboles que están coposos de hojas.

LOS GORRIONES SIENTEN AMOR

Los gorriones sienten amor por sus pichones
como una madre puede sentirlo para sus hijos.
Son las siete de la mañana
y no han podido dar de comer a sus crías:
es cuando andan como locos de jardín en jardín
buscando miel en las flores;
una vez encontrada se lanzan como flechas
hacia donde está el nido.
Los tiernos la quedan viendo,
luego le abren el pico,
ella comienza a darles su desayuno.

EL ALCARAVÁN

El alcaraván canta a las seis de la mañana
y pasa cantando todo el día
da la hora como un reloj.

THE NIGHT BLACK

The night black
crickets sing
foxes howl
while people sleep
in silence
and very early
at three in the morning
you hear the song of the cock
who gives notice when to expect the dawn.

NATALIA SEQUEIRA and Olivia Silva were the only two older residents of Solentiname to participate in the poetry workshop under the supervision of Mayra Jimenez. She is the mother of Elvis Chavarría and lives in the small house where he grew up, near the new Elvis Chavarría School, along with her daughter, the painter Milagros Chavarría.

LA NOCHE NEGRA

La noche negra
los grillos cantan
los zorros chillan
mientras la gente duerme
en el silencio
y en la madrugada se oye
a las tres de la mañana
el cantido de un gallo
que avisa cuando va a amanecer.

ELENA PINEDA

WHEN THE KIDS FROM SOLENTINAME
MADE THE ASSAULT ON SAN CARLOS

The little white and blue boat
color of sky and water
left the dock and one last time
I took a long look at my lovely
archipelago, Solentiname.
That litle group of houses at the edge
of the shore, some
egrets flying below
the grey afternoon sky, the anahinga
eating a fish
under a guava tree,
the zanate jumping and singing,
the güises, the widowbirds, and one moment
I saw them, and the next they were gone.

And at last we leave the lake
and enter the river
toward Costa Rica.
Dusk, in the silence you hear
only the cricket's song
and again I recall the songs
of all the birds of Solentiname
such as the güis with his "Güiiis! Güiiis!"
the pijul with his "Pijul! Pijul! Pijul!"
and the widowbird.

And suddenly I'm jerked awake
by the "pun-pun-pun" the
"traca-traca"
of machine guns in the distance.

ELENA PINEDA is the widow of Laureano Mairena, one of the commanders of the assault on San Carlos. She currently lives in Managua.

CUANDO LOS MUCHACHOS DE SOLENTINAME
ASALTARON SAN CARLOS

El botecito azul y blanco
color de cielo y agua
salió del muelle y por última vez
di un vistazo a mi lindo
archipiélago Solentiname.
Aquel caserillito a la orilla
de la costa, algunas
garzas volando bajo el cielo
gris de la tarde, el pato-aguja
comiendose un pez
debajo de un guabo
el zanate clarinero saltando
los güises, las viudas, y de un
momento a otro ya no vi nada.

Y por fin salimos del lago
entramos al río
hacia Costa Rica.
Anochece, sólo se oye el canto
de los grillos en el silencio
y de nuevo vuelvo
a recordar el canto de
todos los pájaros de Solentiname
como el güis con su güiiis güiiis
el pijul con su pijul, pijul, pijul y la
viuda.

Y de pronto me despertaron
el pun, pun, pun, el traca
traca de las ametralladoras lejanas.

OLIVIA SILVA

12 OCTOBER 1977

It's four o'clock. We have to cross the lake.
Waves, wind, more waves.
To the north, Solentiname fresh and cool
egrets flying toward the great marsh
rice fields being harvested
the cornpatch smelling of sweet new ears of corn,
chattering birds.
And all this, I think,
raped by the National Guard
just as they raped Amada Pineda.

SOLENTINAME

In January we peasants get ready
to bring in the bean crop.

IT'S ALREADY SUMMER

It's already summer and I'm in exile,
I think of the flowering fields of Solentiname.
It's already summer, the madero tree's dangling its long trailing
clusters of pink flowers at the edge of the islands, the helequemes
decorate the water with their orange blossoms, and I
remain in exile.

COSTA RICA

Costa Rica with gardens full of brightly colored flowers
the white and famous calla lily, in doña Emilia's gnarled and twisted
guava tree yigüirros sing all day and
the deep blue color of the sky and
her happy children who have no Guardia to terrorize them.

12 DE OCTUBRE DE 1977

Son las cuatro. Tenemos que irnos a cruzar el lago.
Olas, viento, más olas.
Al norte quedó Solentiname con frescura
garzas volando al Zacatón
arrozales en corta,
milpas con olor a chilote
pájaros chillones.
Y todo eso, pienso yo,
violado por la G.N.
como violaron a Amada Pineda.

SOLENTINAME

En enero los campesinos nos preparamos
a recoger la cosecha de frijoles.

YA ES VERANO

Ya es verano yo estoy en el exilio,
pienso en los campos floridos en Solentiname.
Ya es verano, los maderos con chirriones cubiertos
de flores rosadas a la orilla de las islas, los helequemes
adornan el agua con sus flores anaranjadas, y yo
sigo en el exilio.

COSTA RICA

Costa Rica con jardines llenos de coloridas flores
la famosa y blanca cala, en el retorcido guayabo de
doña Emilia cantan todos los días yigüirros y el
azulito color del cielo y sus niños alegres sin
terror a un guardia.

PAPATURRO

A voyage to Papaturro is something nostalgic.
It's a short river that leaves you with a desire to go on travelling.
It has an abundance of birds such as ibises
egrets bitterns and midget gators and leaf-colored monkeys in summer.

SUMMER AND ITS BEAUTY

In summer the maderos are all full of flowers
that later on become
seed pods.
Its fruit like a bean.
Also helequemes adorn the shores
of Lake Nicaragua.
The high oaks covered with pale purple flowers
make the peasant's sorrowful face
light up for a moment.

IN SOLENTINAME

There's nothing left there in Solentiname,
Ernesto no longer there discussing the Gospels with us,
no more big midday family meals.

Ernesto no longer directs painting in Solentiname.
Only birdsongs remain
and the disgusting presence of Somoza's Guardia.

PAPATURRO

Un viaje a Papaturro es algo nostálgico.
Es un río corto que lo deja a uno con deseo de seguir viajando.
Tiene pájaros en cantidad como cocas
garzas martín-peña guajipales monos color de hoja en el verano.

EL VERANO Y SU BELLEZA

En el verano florecen los maderos
que más tarde se convierten
en vainas.
Su fruto como frijol.
También los helequemes adornan las orillas
del Lago de Nicaragua.
Los altos robles cubiertos de flores lila
alegran la triste mirada
del campesino.

EN SOLENTINAME

En Solentiname allí no ha quedado nada;
no está Ernesto dialogando el Evangelio
con nosotros. Terminó aquel almuerzo en familia.

No está Ernesto dirigiendo las pinturas en Solentiname.
Sólo el canto de los pájaros ha quedado
y la presencia repugnante de la guardia de Somoza.

AT THE TIME OF THE ASSAULT ON THE SAN CARLOS GARRISON

At dusk on the 12th of October we enter
the Rio Guacalito. The howler monkeys shriek to see us go by;
jupati palms and the stench of rotten mud; clouds
of mosquitos biting the kids' faces.

The tension has me on edge, only the song of
crickets and the cry of the oso-caballo who seems to say:
the people will triumph.

SOLENTINAME

My childhood in Solentiname without a school
without even a pair of shoes
and poor nutrition
the same as or worse than other poor Nicaraguan kids.
The best days were during Holy Week
when my mother made us almíbar fruit cup, rosquillas, and pinolillo.
On summer nights the pocoyos would sing
and all day long the cicadas would buzz.

19TH OF MARCH

San José is the Patron Saint of Solentiname
a poor people's fiesta
a Mass celebrated by Ernesto
a communal midday meal
the kids dressed simply
the women in their brightest clothes
doña Angela Rodríguez selling White Rum.

CUANDO EL ASALTO AL CUARTEL DE SAN CARLOS

El 12 de octubre entramos al anochecer
al río Guacalito. Gritan los congos al vernos pasar;
yolillas y olor a lodo podrido: nubes
de zancudos pican las caras de los niños.

Mi tensión es nerviosa, solo el canto de los
grillos y el grito del oso-caballo como diciendo:
el pueblo vencerá.

SOLENTINAME

Mi niñez en Solentiname sin escuela
sin un par de zapatos
y con mala alimentación
igual o peor que otros niños pobres de Nicaragua.
Para semana santa eran los mejores días
cuando mi madre nos preparaba almíbar, rosquillas y pinolillo.
En tiempo de verano por las noches cantaban los pocoyos
y en el día chillaban las chicharras.

19 DE MARZO

San José es el patrono de Solentiname
una fiesta de gentes pobres
una misa celebrada por Ernesto
un almuerzo en común
los niños con ropita sencilla
las mujeres con sus vestidos chillones
doña Angelo Rodríguez vendiendo ron-plata.

THEY CAPTURED DÓNALD AND ELVIS TOGETHER

They captured Dónald and Elvis together
later they were separated
I know they're still alive
which the Guardia denies
but history will absolve them.

THE CHILDREN OF MARCOS JOYA

The children of Marcos Joya are dying for lack of medicine,
there's no school for the son of Ricardo Reyes,
and the old folks can't get enough to eat,
but Somoza has all the newest weapons for killing.

TO MY FOUR SONS UP IN THE MOUNTAINS

The kids in the mountains
have no blankets
they sleep on the ground
huddled close to their comrades
on winter nights
the tall wet grass
soaks their weary bodies;
and unlike the Guardia
nobody brings them
lunch by helicopter.
But by risking their lives
they'll give to other Nicaraguans
those quilts and that lunch.

A DÓNALD Y ELVIS LOS CAPTURARON JUNTOS

A Dónald y Elvis los capturaron juntos
más tarde los separaron
yo sé que están vivos y que la guardia los niega,
pero la historia los absolverá.

LOS HIJOS DE MARCOS JOYA

Los hijos de Marcos Joya mueren sin medicina,
escuelas no hay para lo de Ricardo Reyes,
ni los ancianos pueden alimentarse
pero Somoza tiene armas modernísimas para matar.

A MIS CUATRO HIJOS EN LA MONTAÑA

Ellos en la montaña
no tienen cobijas
junto a sus compañeros
en el suelo duermen
el zacate mojado
en las noches de invierno
moja sus cuerpos cansados;
y almuerzo en helicóptero
no les llega
como a la guardia.
Pero ellos con sus vidas
darán a otros en Nicaragua
esas colchas y ese almuerzo.

ARCHIPELAGO OF GREEN ISLANDS

Archipelago of green islands
with flocks of ducks diving in stony coves
under thick-leaved guava trees.
In May the güises build their nests,
when the first rains come torches glow at night
and we start to plant our corn.
The days are calm,
it is very hot.

OLIVIA SILVA, matriarch of the Guevara clan (her children represented in this book include Dónald, Gloria, Iván, Myriam, Alejandro, Esperanza, William, and Mariita) is a respected painter. These days she lives mainly in Managua, where she conducts painting classes in the prisons.

ARCHIPIÉLAGO DE VERDES ISLAS

Archipiélago de verdes islas
con bandadas de patos buceando junto a los corrales de piedra
bajo los frondosos guabos.
En mayo los güises construyen sus nidos
con las primeras lluvias brillan en la noche los hachones
y se comienza a sembrar el maíz.
Los días son calmos
hace mucho calor.

EDDY CHAVARRÍA

THE FISHERMAN

The fisherman with his pole
his hook and his boat
has to leave.
She, his wife, at the tip
of the stone jetty
leaning against a guava tree
keeps her eyes fixed on him.

IT'S SUMMER

It's summer
and the time I have left
to stay in Solentiname
is running out.
The winds bring me bitter memory
of years that will not return.
Time goes by
just as flocks go by — doves,
ducks, parrots, pigeons.
The nights go by fast
and I shudder to think
I have to leave my land.

IN EVERY HOLLOW

In every hollow
you're aware of a world
completely full
surrounded by nature.
Sometimes you hear the throaty rasp
of an oropéndola who moves
from tree to tree
in search of his livelihood.

EL PESCADOR

El pescador con su palanca
su anzuelo y su bote
tiene que partir.
Ella, su mujer en la punta
del muelle de piedra
arrecostada a un árbol de guabo
lo queda viendo.

ES VERANO

Es verano
y el tiempo que me queda
de estar en Solentiname
se está agotando.
Los vientos me traen amargo recuerdo
de años que no volverán.
El tiempo sigue pasando
como pasan las bandadas de palomas
patos, loras, piches.
Las noches se me hacen cortas
y me estremezco al pensar
que tengo que dejar mi tierra.

EN CADA RINCÓN

En cada rincón
se siente un mundo
todo lleno
rodeado de la naturaleza.
A veces se escucha el garraspeo
de una oropéndola que va
de palo en palo
buscando su vida.

WINTER

Winter comes singing
with its downpours and its gales.
It clothes roads, trees and mountains,
amazing with its colors.
The lake swallows up its stone harbors,
the shores grow narrow.
The evenings are grey, quiet.
The nights are black.

SEATED IN THE DOORWAY

Seated in the doorway
I let my eyes run over
the mountains and the roads
dried up by time.
Only a dog goes by
with a hangdog look.
The day peters out
and I go on waiting.

THE MOON HAS ALREADY SET

The moon has already set.
Dawn will soon be over.
Then up on that mountain chilled by the mist
the sun bringing no hope
to the fisherman.

INVIERNO

El invierno viene cantando
con sus chaparrones y vendavales.
Viste caminos árboles y montañas
impresionando con su colorido.
El lago se traga los corrales de piedra,
las costas se estrechan.
Las tardes son grises, silenciosas.
Las noches son negras.

SENTADO EN LA PUERTA

Sentado en la puerta
corro la mirada
en las montañas y caminos
asolados por el tiempo.
Sólo un perro camina
con la mirada baja.
El día se agotó
y yo sigo esperando.

LA LUNA YA SE OCULTÓ

La luna ya se ocultó.
El alba pronto se irá.
Y en aquella montaña fría por la niebla
el sol sin esperanzas
para el pescador.

WHEN THE TREES BEGIN TO DROP THEIR LEAVES

When the trees begin to drop their leaves
and the lake starts to dry up
parched by the exhausting sun
and when the roads are turned into
dusty lanes
and when as you pass by
every farmhouse
you smell the odor of hot rosquillas,
cornmeal pies,
that's when Holy Week
has arrived in Solentiname.

THE GARROBOS

The garrobos at the tip
of a dead branch
warm themselves in the midday sun.
The mangos and oranges
rock
back and forth
in the hum of the wind
and over there at the tip of an island
waves are breaking where
farther on
in a protected cove
you find a plain straw farmhouse
which serves as an emblem
of the humble condition
of its inhabitants.

CUANDO LOS ÁRBOLES EMPIEZAN A BOTAR LAS HOJAS

Cuando los árboles empiezan a botar las hojas
y el lago a consecuencia de los agotadores soles
comienza a secar,
y cuando los caminos se convierten
en callejones polvosos,
y cuando en cada rancho
al pasar cerca
se siente el olor a rosquillas calientes,
empanaditas de maíz,
es cuando en Solentiname
ha llegado la Semana Santa.

LOS GARROBOS

Los garrobos a la punta
de un palo seco
calientan en el sol de medio día.
Los mangos y naranjos
se mecen
continuamente
con el zumbar del viento
y allá en la punta de una isla
las olas se rompen donde
más adelante
en una ensenada muy mansa
se encuentra un ranchito
de paja,
muy natural,
que sirve para pintar la humildad
de sus habitantes.

THE BIRDS SING

The birds sing.
The almond trees sway.
The güises announce the morning sun.
Roses, you can smell them everywhere.
The farmhands with their machetes
get ready for a new day.
The hens are already flapping down from the branches.
The milkman on his way to the village
trots by with his horse.
But me, I'm unhappy:
you never came.

EDDY CHAVARRÍA, younger brother of Elvis, lives in San Carlos.

LOS PÁJAROS CANTAN

Los pájaros cantan.
Los almendros se mecen.
Los güises anuncian el sol de la mañana.
Las rosas se sienten en el ambiente.
Los peones con sus machetes
se disponen a un nuevo día.
Las gallinas ya vienen bajando de los palos.
El lechero que va al pueblo
pasa al trote con su caballo.
Pero yo estoy triste,
vos no llegaste.

JULIA CHAVARRÍA

THE LETTER

When I took your letter
in my hand, I didn't know
whether to read it or not.

JULIA CHAVARRÍA lives in Solentiname.

LA CARTA

Cuando tomé tu carta
en mi mano, no supe
si leerla o no.

IRENE AGUDELO

THE CLOUDS

The clouds are grey.
The air.
The yellow flowers.
The painted houses,
                    and the trees.

THE LITTLE CHOCOYO

One day early in the morning
I know what the little chocoyo said:
                    I want ripe mangos.
                    I want ripe mangos.

IRENE AGUDELO was five years old when she wrote these poems. Her parents helped Ernesto Cardenal form the community in Solentiname, where Irene was born.

LAS NUBES

Las nubes están grises.
El aire.
Y las flores amarillas.
Las casas pintadas,
                              y los árboles.

EL CHOCOYITO

Un día muy de mañanita
sé que dijo el chocoyito:
                    quiero mangos maduros
                    quiero mangos maduros.

JOSÉ RAMÓN MENESES

IN LAKE NICARAGUA

In Lake Nicaragua
the boats go by breaking waves
as though they were tractors.
And when a tarpon
jumps
you see it glisten as though it were made of silver.

DUSK

The wind blows, the waves smash on the shore
the sun drops out of sight on the blue horizon.
The egrets hurry off to catch sardines.
When the wind gets worse the egrets get worried.
Bit by bit the sun goes down.

THE TREES MOVE

The trees move with the
blowing of the icy wind
that runs through this place.
The parrots sing for happiness
and the swallows circle
in the air
and the waves in the morning
break
as though greeting you and
the güises greet
the new day
singing.

JOSÉ RAMÓN MENESES was 10 years old when he wrote these poems. He
was then the kid brother of Pedro Pablo Meneses.

184

EN EL LAGO DE NICARAGUA

En el lago de Nicaragua
pasan botes rompiendo olas
como si fueran tractores.
Y cuando un sábalo real
salta
se ve brillar como si fuera de plata.

UN ATARDECER

El viento sopla, las olas revientan
el sol se oculta en el horizonte azul.
Las garzas se aligeran a cazar sardinas.
Cuando el viento se arrecia las garzas se afligen.
El sol va bajando poco a poco.

LOS ÁRBOLES SE MUEVEN

Los árboles se mueven con el
brisar del viento helado
que corre por este lugar.
Las loras cantan de alegría
y las golondrinas revolotean
en el aire
y las olas en la mañana
revientan
como saludando a uno y
los güises saludan
al día nuevo
cantando.

MAURICIO CHAVARRÍA

I SAW A TURTLE IN THE LAKE

I saw a turtle in the lake.
He was swimming by
and I was going by in a sailboat.

THE CHOCOYO

One day I went up the mountain
and I saw a mango tree
and a chocoyo eating a ripe mango
and my mouth began to water
and I climbed the tree and started to pick mangos.

MAURICIO CHAVARRÍA was a 10-year-old Solentiname kid when he wrote
these poems.

YO VÍ UNA TORTUGA EN EL LAGO

Yo ví una tortuga en el lago.
Iba nadando
y yo iba en un bote de vela.

EL CHOCOYO

Un día fui al monte
y vi un palo de mango
y un chocoyo comiéndose un mango maduro
y se me hizo agua la boca
y me subí al palo a cortar mangos.

JONNY CHAVARRÍA

CAMPESINOS

The campesinos work.
The rich watch the poor suffer.
While the campesinos eat beans
the rich eat meat every day and
whatever else they want.
You see the poor folks with ragged clothes
but the rich wear nylon clothes.
The poor live in houses made of cardboard boxes
and the exploiters laugh at the campesinos.

HAPPY

I feel happy because I have my parents.
I feel happy because I know how to read.
And I feel happy because I am a poet.

JONNY CHAVARRÍA was 11 when he wrote these poems.

CAMPESINO

El campesino trabaja.
Los ricos ven al pobre sufrir.
Mientras el campesino come frijoles
el rico carne todos los días y
lo que quieran.
El pobre se viste con ropas rajadas
el rico se viste con ropas diolén.
El pobre vive en casas de cartón
y los explotadores se ríen del campesino.

FELIZ

Feliz me siento porque tengo a mis padres.
Feliz me siento porque sé leer.
Y feliz me siento porque soy poeta.

JUAN AGUDELO

THE MALINCHE

On the island of Mancarrón
there is a leafy malinche
with branches full of flowers
yellow, black and orange;
and some butterflies
orange, black and yellow
sucking sweet nectar,
and the güis — yellow breast, coffee-colored back —
eating butterflies.

THIS POEM IS FOR THE SWALLOWS ON A VERY SAD WINTER DAY

In winter the swallows go around announcing that
the rain is coming.
Now they are happier than we are, the little swallows,
but later we will be happier than they are
because we'll have lots of ripe fruit here in Solentiname.
Ah, the rain has begun, what happiness for the trees.
Already the first drops are falling, the swallows are going away.

THE POEM

Poetry is born in a sacuanjoche blossom
in which red butterflies suck nectar.
Poetry is what two lovers
say to one another.
Poetry is more delicate than the reflection of the moon in the lake.
A perfect poem is like the Revolution.

EL MALINCHE

En la isla de Mancarrón
hay un malinche frondoso
con las ramas llenas de flores
de color amarillo, negro y anaranjado;
y unas mariposas
anaranjadas, negras y amarillas
chupando miel dulce,
y el güis pecho amarillo, espalda café
comiendo mariposas.

ESTE POEMA ES PARA LAS GOLONDRINAS
EN UN DÍA MUY TRISTE DE INVIERNO

En el invierno las golondrinas andan diciendo la noticia de que va a
venir la lluvia.
Ahora están más alegres que nosotros las pequeñas golondrinas,
pero después nosotros estaremos más que ellas,
porque en Solentiname vamos a tener muchas frutas maduras.
Ah, empezó la lluvia, qué alegría para los palos.
Ya están cayendo las primeras gotas, las golondrinas se están alejando.

EL POEMA

La poesía nace en una flor de sacuanjoche
en la que mariposas rojas chupan el néctar.
La poesía son las cosas que se dicen
un par de enamorados.
La poesía es más delicada que el reflejo de la luna
en el lago.
Un poema perfecto es como la Revolución.

THE REVOLUTION IS

The Revolution is Fidel Castro playing basketball
The Revolution is the Granma in which all the heroes travel
The Revolution is Sandino giving a speech to his people
The Revolution is that all the mamas take good care of their children
The Revolution is a lake where there are fish for everyone
The Revolution is a couple in love
The Revolution is a sacuanjoche blossom
The Revolution is Mario Ávila putting a poem to music
The Revolution is a cannonball shot at the imperialists
The Revolution is beating the imperialists
The Revolution is Ernesto Cardenal writing a poem for Solentiname
The Revolution is a brightly colored butterfly that
        flies all around the heroes
The Revolution is all the Cubans applauding Fidel
The Revolution is my papa making a sculpture with all its
        different shapes.

JUAN AGUDELO, like his sister Irene, was born on Solentiname. He was
seven years old when he wrote these poems. These days his specialty is
harvesting coffee.

LA REVOLUCIÓN ES

La Revolución es Fidel Castra jugando basket-ball
La Revolución es el Granma donde viajaron los héroes
La Revolución es Sandino diciendo un discurso a su pueblo
La Revolución es que todas las mamás cuiden bien a sus niños
La Revolución es el lago donde hay pescados para todos
La Revolución es una pareja de enamorados
La Revolución es la flor de sacuanjoche
La Revolución es Mario Ávila poniéndole música a un poema
La Revolución es una bola de cañon que dispara a los imperialistas
La Revolución es vencer a los imperialistas
La Revolución es Ernesto Cardenal escribiendo un poema
        para Solentiname
La Revolución es una mariposa de colores que pasa volando
        alrededor de los héroes
La Revolución son todos los cubanos aplaudiendo a Fidel
La Revolución es mi papá haciendo una escultura con todos
        sus formones.

Appendix

APPENDIX:

Four additional poems by Bosco Centeno, from his first book, *Puyonearon los granos*, winner of the 1981 Leonel Rugama Prize.

LETTER TO MAYRA

I write you from Solentiname where I'm on vacation.
Outside, the wind whips the leaves from the trees
and carries them toward the shore, which goes all white.

In this month of January a strong wind blows from the Chontales hills.
I went back today to the places we used to hold our Poetry Workshops
and I remembered Felipe bringing his poems
which he'd dig out of his pockets on crumpled sheets of paper
as though they were money
and when we thought he had none left he'd rummage in his pockets
and find another
(and we'd never know if that was really the last poem).

I could remember as well the places
where we read poets under the mangos —
we read Gioconda and Whitman in the alleyway of trees
and those Chinese and Japanese poets we were so fond of.
Do you remember that someone said,
"How wonderful it would be to write poetry so closely tied
to the life of the people as this, so that someday all documents
would be poems — even an I.O.U."?

How we admired the poet Silva with his waterfowl
and vigilant Indians!
And the poet Coronel! We came to know Ernesto as a poet,
and so many others; and this memory
and the lake bring you to my mind, Mayra:
I see you in your boat built here in the workshops,
steering between the waves of this raging lake
with the certainty that you and your boat would arrive safely
at that port on this island we dreamt of for our people.

CARTA A MAYRA

Te escribo desde Solentiname, donde estoy de vacaciones.
Afuera el viento arrastra las hojas de los árboles
y las lleva hacia la playa, que blanquea.

En este mes de enero sopla un fuerte viento de las costas de Chontales.
Hoy recorrí los lugares donde hacíamos los Talleres de Poesía
y recordé a Felipe llevando sus poemas,
que siempre sacaba del pantalón en papeles arrugados,
como si fuera dinero,
y cuando creíamos que no tenía más, rebuscaba en sus bolsillos
y encontraba otro.
(Nunca sabíamos si era en realidad el último.)

Pude recordar, además, los lugares
donde leíamos a los poetas, bajo los palos de mango;
leíamos a la Gioconda y a Whitman en el corredor,
a los poetas chinos y japoneses que tanto nos gustaron.
¿Recordás que alguien dijo:
"qué lindo sería que se escribiera poesía tan popular como esa,
y que todos los documentos algún día fueran poemas,
hasta los cobros"?

¡Cómo nos gustó el poeta Silva, con sus piches
y con sus indios en la vela,
y el poeta Coronel! Conocimos a Ernesto como poeta
y a tantos más; y ese recuerdo
y el lago me hacen imaginarte, Mayra,
en tu bote construido en los Talleres
navegando entre las olas de este lago embravecido,
con la certeza de que llegarás con tu bote
al puerto que soñamos para nuestro pueblo en esta isla.

DÓNALD

My brother-in-law Dónald was shy and elusive like a mojarra;
he fought like a tiger that 13th of October in San Carlos;
he liked to visit the girls on the opposite shore
with his outboard motor on the boat he had built himself.
The Guardia murdered him along with Elvis there on the banks
        of the Rio Frío;
and he used to dream of the cooperatives and the schools
that now bear his name.

TO ELVIS CHAVARRÍA

It's not with your guitar that we'll remember you,
giving serenades on moonlit nights
on the nearby islands,
nor with your uncommon skill in sports,
nor with your wooden pole fishing on Isla del Padre
nor stopping iguanas dead in their tracks with a well-aimed stone.
We'll remember you, brother,
in the laughter of the children of Oscar, of Pocho, of Chica,
who run and laugh fit and healthy
across the open fields of our fatherland.

DÓNALD

Dónald, mi cuñado, era arisco como una mojarra,
peleó como un tigre el trece de octubre en San Carlos,
le gustaba visitar a las muchachas en la
costa de enfrente con su motor fuera de borda
en el bote que él construyó.
La guardia lo asesinó junto a Elvis en la ribera del Río Frío;
y soñaba con las cooperativas y las escuelas
que hoy llevan su nombre.

A ELVIS CHAVARRÍA

No vamos a recordarte con tu guitarra
en las noches de luna, poniendo serenatas
en las islas vecinas.
Ni con tu agilidad poco común en los deportes,
ni pescando con tu vara de madroño
en la Isla del Padre,
ni cazando iguanas a certeras pedradas.
Te vamos a recordar, hermano,
en la risa de los hijos de Oscar, de Pocho, de la Chica,
que corren y ríen sanos
por los rastrojos de la patria.

FELIPE PEÑA

Your song, brother, can be heard
in the chorchas, güises and trumpeting zanates
who sing in the open fields along the rivers,
disturbed by campesinos hard at work today cutting and clearing
        their land,
or frightened by the splash of paddles
and the songs of kids
going downstream to teach reading and writing

in the roar of the jaguar in the mountains
who almost seems to be demanding back those guardatinajas and deer
you beat him to
and that you cooked to perfection
in the guerrilla camp
there in the humid, mosquito-filled hills along the Rio San Juan

in those nights when we hear the sad song of the oso-caballo
and remember you on those moonlit nights
standing near the lean-to
the moon glinting off the lean-to
like a slice of our lake
and you speaking of Solentiname cooperatives
and of the girls you immortalized in your poems
and remembered in those songs you sang to the sound of your guitar.

Your song is in the steady rain
of San Juan del Norte
and is fused with that picture of you that afternoon in camp —
the heroic guerrillero

with your rifle and backpack,
like a partisan poster,
ready to set off into the mountains of Nueva Guinea,

with that Indian look of yours,
contemplating the future,

and your smile
and your shout: "¡Patria Libre o Morir!"

FELIPE PEÑA

Tu canto, hermano, puede oírse
en las chorchas, güises y zanates clarineros
que cantan en las vegas de los ríos
alborotados por la derriba de los campesinos
que hoy trabajan su tierra,
o espantados por canaletes,
y los cantos de los muchachos
que bajan el río para alfabetizar,

en el bramido del tigre en la montaña
que pareciera reclamar las guardatinajas y los venados
que vos le disputabas
y tan sabroso cocinaste
en el campamento guerrillero
en las montañas húmedas y zancudosas del San Juan.

En las noches con el canto triste del oso-caballo,
con tu recuerdo en esas noches con luna
junto a las champas,
reflejándose la luna en la champa
como un trozo de nuestro lago,
hablando de las cooperativas de Solentiname
y de las muchachas a las que perpetuaste en tus poemas
y que recordaste con canciones
que te acompañabas con tu guitarra.
Tu canto está en la lluvia constante
de San Juan del Norte,

con tu imagen de guerrillero altivo y heroico
de aquella tarde en el campamento,

con tu fusil y mochila como póster
del comité de solidaridad
al partir a la montaña de Nueva Guinea,

con tu mirada de indio
como atisbando el futuro,

con la sonrisa
y tu grito de Patria Libre o Morir.

Glossary

GLOSSARY

AGUDELO(S): In 1966 Colombian poet William Agudelo helped Ernesto Cardenal found a religious commune in Solentiname. Later his wife Teresita joined him. Their children Juan and Irene were both born in Solentiname.

AGOUTI: A burrowing rodent of the genus *Dasyprocta;* called "guatuza" in Nicaragua.

ALMÍBAR: In Solentiname, a sweetened fruit cup.

BARBUDO: A small "bearded" fish, member of the catfish family, six to eight inches long.

CEIBA: Large Central American tree, sacred to the Maya.

CHAYULE(S): Fruit flies or gnats that swarm in great clouds.

CHIGÜINES (LOS): "The Kids," the name of Somoza's crack battalion.

CHILAMATE: A tree, member of the *ficus* family.

CHILATE: A drink based on toasted corn and water to which chile and chocolate are added.

CHOCOYO: A kind of parakeet; it flies in noisy flocks around Solentiname.

CHORCHA: An oriole, notable for its beautiful yellow color, for its song, and for its nests that dangle from trees.

CHOSCHOS: A small flycatcher, colored like the güis; its name is onomatopoetic of its song (Nicaraguan pronunciation usually drops the terminal *s*): "cho-cho-cho-cho."

CLARINERO: The male zanate.

CORTÉS DE LA CIGÜEÑA: "In Nicaragua a characteristic tree is the cortés (*Tecoma sideroxylon*) yielding timber as hard as ebony, and noteworthy for the golden blossoms with which it is entirely covered after the leaves have fallen." —*Encyclopedia Britannica.*

DELICIAS: A town in Costa Rica.

ELEQUEME: Also "helequeme." A common Central American tree with orange blossoms. Also known as "bucaré."

ESCAZÚ: A barrio of San José, Costa Rica, traditional home to Nicaraguan refugees.

ESPERANZA, LA: A hacienda near the Río Frío owned by Somoza where Elvis Chavarría and Dónald Guevara were killed and buried.

GARROBO: An iguana-like lizard native to Nicaragua, prized for its delicate white flesh.

GENERAL OF FREE MEN, THE: An epithet for Sandino.

GENÍZARO: One of the largest trees in Nicaragua, with a corpulent, elephantine base; a favorite shade tree.

GRANMA: The boat on which Fidel Castro and his followers sailed to
    Cuba to begin the insurrection against Fulgencio Batista.
GUACIMÓN: A tree, *Guazuma ulmifolia*.
GUAIRON(ES): A fish-eating bird.
GUANACASTE: *Enterolobium cyclocarpum*. "They often stand alone and are
    very handsome trees with trunks three to four feet in diameter
    and immense spread of branches. The head is as large as our
    spreading oak but the spray is more graceful and lacks the stiff
    ruggedness of the oak. The guanacaste is a mimosa with a
    much divided leaf as fine and delicate as a maidenhair fern."
    —A.S. and P.P. Calvert, *A Year of Costa Rican Natural History*,
    1917.
GUAPOTE: A freshwater fish common in Lake Nicaragua.
GUÁS: A songbird; also makes a raucous cry.
GÜIS(ES): The Great Kiskadee, a large flycatcher with bright yellow
    breast and an extraordinarily beautiful song.
HELEQUEME: Elequeme.
LA BARTOLINA: A prison in San Carlos.
LIBERALES: The Partido Liberal Nacionalista was Tacho Somoza's party.
LUIS ALFONSO VELÁSQUEZ: Luis was a nine-year-old boy who played an
    active role in the Revolution as a Sandinista collaborator and
    organizer of children. He was killed by the Guardia before the
    final victory in July of 1979. The Associaciones de Niños
    Sandinistas Luis Alfonso Velásquez are named after him. Thus,
    "those Luis Alfonso Velásquezes" would be either members of
    one of the clubs or children who emulate his example.
MADERO: A kind of tree.
MADROÑO: Madrone, *Arbutus*.
MALINCHE: A colorful flowering bush.
MILPA: A crude field prepared for planting by the slash-and-burn
    method.
MOJARRA: Also spelled "moharra." Freshwater fish of the *Cichlidae*
    family. Looks like a cross between a bream and a sheepshead;
    excellent eating; caught by fishing *through* the dense lakeside
    vegetation of zacate and sontole, using small crabs as bait.
MONIMBÓ: An Indian barrio in Masaya, site of the first important up-
    rising against Somoza.
NICOLASA, LA: A paramilitary terrorist who served under Somoza; she
    was known for her ruthlessness.

NISPERO: A fruit, comparable to zapote or sapodilla.

NUEVA GUINEA: A settlement in the mountains northeast of San Carlos.

OSO-CABALLO: A member of the fox family, with a long furry tail; more often heard than seen.

OROPÉNDOLA: A large coffee-colored bird with streaks of dazzling yellow in its tail.

PALOMETA: A Nicaraguan lake fish.

PIJUL: A songbird; the name is onomatopoetic of its call: "pijul! pijul!"

PINOL(ILLO): A drink similar to chilate, of cornmeal base, to which various other ingredients are added; also, the flour of toasted maize, sometimes baked with meat or used to thicken gravy as in a "pinol de iguana."

PITAHAYA, PITAYA: *Cereus pitajaya*, a cactus with red flowers and edible fruit; grows on the limbs of trees and on rooftops.

POCOLLO, POCOYO: A small nocturnal bird, *Antrostomus vociferus*, that sings along roadsides.

POROPORO: A large tree that has bright yellow spring flowers before it grows leaves.

PUNCO: A fish-eating bittern or heron. According to doña Olivia Silva, when the punco sings softly, "groo . . . groo . . . ," the weather will be calm; when it sings more quickly, "gro-gro-gro," strong wind is on the way; when it sings stridently, "cho! cho! cho! cho!" it's going to rain.

ROSQUILLA: A sweet, tough pastry made of interlocking rings.

SACUANJOCHE: A tree with white flowers, the national flower of Nicaragua.

SAN CARLOS: A garrison town at the southeastern end of Lake Nicaragua. The temporarily successful assault on the San Carlos garrison in October of 1977 resulted in the deaths of Elvis Chavarría and Dónald Guevara, the imprisonment of Felipe Peña and the subsequent destruction of the Solentiname commune by the National Guard. Surviving members of the community fled to Costa Rica.

SAN JUAN DE LA CRUZ: Name of the boat used by the Solentiname rebels in their attack on the San Carlos garrison.

SAN NICOLÁS, LITTLE DOVE OF: A very small dove, like an Inca dove.

SENZONTLE: A mockingbird, *Mimus gilvus*, with a short beak and a melodious song; from the Aztec word "cenzontlatolle."

SONZONATE: Also spelled "sonsonate." A flowering tree; also the name of a province in El Salvador.

TACHO: Nickname for Anastasio Somoza Debayle.

TARPON: In Nicaragua called "Sábalo Real," often mistranslated as "shad," to which it is related. Lake Nicaragua record stands at 120 pounds.

TIQUISQUE: Sometimes also called "quequisque." An edible root similar to yucca.

VIRGIN: "The image of the Virgin." —Kent Johnson, *A Nation of Poets*.

WIDOWBIRD: "Viuda." The blue tanager, *Thraupsis episcopus*.

YIGÜIRRO(S): A songbird, *Turdus grayi*; national bird of Costa Rica.

ZANATE: A grackle-family bird, *Quiscalus macrourus*, that digs up and eats newly planted corn in a slash-and-burn milpa. The male is called "clarinero" ("bugler").

Short Bibliography

SHORT BIBLIOGRAPHY

Arcia, Nubia, et al. *El asalto a San Carlos*. Managua: Ministerio de
    Cultura, 1982.
Cardenal, Ernesto. *The Gospel in Solentiname*. Maryknoll, NY: Orbis
    Books, 1979. 4 vols.
———*Vuelos de Victoria/Flights of Victory*. Introduction by Marc Zimmer-
    man. Maryknoll, NY: Orbis Books, 1985.
Centeno, Bosco. *Puyonearon los granos*. Managua: Ministerio de Cultura,
    1983.
Jimenez, Mayra, ed. *Poesia campesina de Solentiname*. Managua:
    Ministerio de Cultura, 1983.
Johnson, Kent, ed. & trans. *A Nation of Poets*. Includes an interview
    with Ernesto Cardenal. Los Angeles: West End Press, 1985.
La Duke, Betty. *Compañeras: Women, Art and Social Change in Latin
    America*. San Francisco: City Lights Books, 1985.
Randall, Margaret. *Risking a Somersault in the Air: Conversations with
    Nicaraguan Writers*. San Francisco: Solidarity Publications, 1984.